SHIFT

THE

FIELD

ALSO BY DARLA LEDOUX

Retreat and Grow Rich: The Entrepreneur's
Guide to Profitable, Powerful Retreats

SHIFT
THE
FIELD

HOW TO DELIVER THE TRANSFORMATION
YOUR CLIENTS CRAVE WHILE UNLOCKING
THE MAGIC YOU WERE BORN TO SHARE

DARLA LEDOUX

WORLDCHANGERS
M E D I A

Edited by Bryna Haynes / www.TheAuthorRevolution.com

Cover art by Veronica Wirth / www.Evolvative.com

Layout by Ivica Jandrijević / www.WritingNights.org

Author Photographs by Kimmi Ward / www.BigMissionStudios.com

ISBN 978-0-9993991-2-5 (Perfect bound)
978-0-9993991-3-2 (eBook)

Published by WorldChangers Media
PO Box 83, Foster, RI 02825
www.WorldChangers.Media

WORLDCHANGERS
MEDIA

PEOPLE ARE SAYING ...

"*Shift the Field* is for the coach or consultant who has tried every tool and trick in the book, and still feels frustrated with client results. The perspective, frameworks, and tools in this book will give you a new way of looking at and supporting transformational change. It centers your clients' truth, and puts you in a more grounded, effective role, leading to breakthrough results."
— **Pamela Slim, author,** *Body of Work*

"Darla is masterful at creating transformational experiences and breaking down the processes that one must go through in order to lead others effectively toward their greatest growth. Her fierce commitment to supporting people to find their own magic and live it fully means her teachings don't force you to live in someone else's box but to live a truly Sourced experience following *your* life path of service."
— **Katherine Bird, Mentor for Healing Practitioners**

"A great coach doesn't give you answers, but helps you access your own. *Shift the Field* takes this to a whole new level, offering today's coaches, healers and teachers a 'revelationary' framework that can be used to achieve repeatable breakthrough results. In essence, Darla gives us a key that opens the portal into practical magic, and reveals the secret ingredient we need for quantum results every time—the divine energy of Source."
— **Monica Rodgers, founder, The Revelation Project**

"Darla is a master of her craft, and in this book reveals the true heart of transformation: your *energy*. Through detailed stories and an easy-to-understand framework, she has made fulfilling and sustainable success accessible to anyone who truly wants this kind of transformation for themselves, as well as for those who want to facilitate it for others."
— **Lisa Berkovitz, Soul Mastery Coach**

"*Shift the Field* is a must-read for any coach who wishes to truly help their clients transform. It provides easy-to-understand steps and fascinating examples of real client situations to illustrate a unique methodology, which involves tapping into an individual's energetic field to get their desired outcome."
— **Janet Newman, Ph.D., author of *Living in the Chemical Age***

"Transformation is the most powerful catalyst for personal joy and growth. Darla masterfully takes the concept of transformation—which can often feel nebulous—and provides a solid framework for how transformation looks and feels, and how a transformational leader can facilitate this process. The ability to lead transformationally is a powerful gift and skill set that, when adopted by wider audiences, can play an important role in global healing. Any coach, consultant, or leader who desires to be a part of this global shift will benefit from reading this book."
— **Amber Swenor, Transformational Life and Business Strategist at Soul Seed**

"This beautifully-written book, full of tangible and recognizable stories, is for all teachers, leaders, and practitioners who work with the intention of facilitating deep transformation. As LeDoux points out, many people have elements of what she calls 'The Anatomy of Transformation,' but their results with clients suffer because they don't have all the elements or understand how to have them work together. This gem will inspire, inform, and delight those wanting to take their work to another level—to transform their practices and themselves in partnership with Source."
— **Maggie Ostara, PhD, Human Design specialist at SovereigntybyDesign.com, mentor, speaker, and author**

"I've been in the professional coaching world since 1999, and I have to say, there are few people who can do what Darla LeDoux does. Put simply, Darla knows how to create transformation—real, deep and meaningful change—for her clients. People make powerful shifts in her presence. It's easy to think that this is 'magic,' or something special that only Darla can do, but the truth is we can *all* learn to do this for ourselves and our clients. The *Shift the Field* approach that Darla shares in this book lays it out for us in a clear, loving, and actionable way. I am recommending this book to anyone who wants to be a part of the transformation that we so dearly need in our world today."
— **Tina Forsyth, leadership coach, founder of Certified OBM**

DEDICATION

This book is dedicated to all of my teachers—
those who taught through supportive containers,
and those who taught through contrast.

Thank you for my growth.

TABLE OF CONTENTS

INTRODUCTION

I sat in the center of a circle with tears streaming down my cheeks, anxiously awaiting my fate.

Was I telling the Truth? I thought so, but I wasn't sure.

I was in my early twenties, a few years into my career as a Senior Product Development Engineer at Procter & Gamble. I loved my job. I was proud of what I'd accomplished, having grown up in a small town with blue collar parents. I thought I knew what I was doing with my life, and that I was "making it" in the world.

But then, this happened.

I was nominated for an immersive training to become a "diversity coach" within my company. The role was to support coworkers to get their potential biases about one another out on the table early on, before unhealthy patterns could develop. In order to facilitate these conversations about beliefs that are often hidden from our view, it was critical that each of us could look within and bring to light our own belief systems. We had to tell the truth to ourselves about the beliefs we'd created or inherited so we could be unbiased space holders.

We received loads of cultural training and various personal assessments, but the crux of this training was the Fishbowl, a powerful exercise developed by Patricia Pope. In the Fishbowl, each person sits in the center of a circle of other humans from all levels of the organization and shares their personal beliefs about race, gender, sexual orientation, and age (one Bowl for each category). The people on the outside of the circle then give a thumbs-up or thumbs-down to indicate whether they believe you are telling the Truth.

Thanks to my training as an engineer, I primarily relied on logical thinking to make my way in life. I'd never talked a lot about myself before—never mind explored how my experiences in life were shaping the way I viewed and interacted with my world. My anxiety around being the center of attention and speaking with such vulnerability caused my body to break down in unexpected ways—to the point where I ended up in the emergency room the night before I was to enter the Bowl.

So there I was, shaking and terrified, having just shared my judgments about men and women from the perspective of a child from a broken home ... but I had lived. Not only that, I'd passed. I'd been telling the Truth—a Truth I never knew existed before that weekend.

As we navigated day after day of this exercise in our group of twenty-four (which equaled ninety-six Fishbowls!) I began to feel more and more nervous—and, at the same time, more and more alive. I felt like I'd been punched in the gut. I was struggling to breathe, feeling parts of myself I had no idea existed.

Although I didn't know it in that moment, transformation had just become the study of my life.

I'd never before understood the profound impact my parents' divorce—and the resulting conflicts which I'd been forced to navigate at far too early an age—had had on me. I always maintained that I was "fine," and that the experience hadn't affected me. What a grand pretense!

But my breakthroughs weren't confined to my own experience. As I observed my colleagues in the center of the circle, I saw how easily our group could discern whether someone was telling the Truth, and I began to wonder why we rarely used this superpower in our day-to-day life. Why was it so challenging for us as humans to actually be present to, and share the Truth? I could immediately see how little Truth was being spoken in our conversations at work. We had the meeting-before-the-meeting to get on the same page so no one ever had to risk speaking their truth in front of their colleagues.

If we were pretending and avoiding Truth so assiduously in my organization, how was this affecting all of our lives? And since the people I worked with couldn't possibly be the only ones doing this, how was this "truth aversion" playing out in our society as a whole?

Why didn't everybody know about this?

Why wasn't our personal Truth the standard to which we held everything?

That question has never left me. In fact, it's the reason I'm writing this book.

SEEING A NEW TRUTH

My days in the Fishbowl changed everything about how I interacted with my world. I became a voracious student of all things transformation. For the first time, I observed the patterns that had taken hold in my life as a result of my past experiences. I saw how I brought those same patterns into new life situations, new roles, and new relationships. And I learned, painstakingly, how to transform these old wounds and frustrations into new energy and fresh results.

I read books, attended trainings on transformational modalities, and tried out new approaches at home and at work. And while it took me ten years and two more careers to get there—I was a high school math teacher and a brand marketer—I eventually followed the seed that had been planted in my heart at that original training and hung my shingle as a coach.

This move seemed insane for a long time. After all, I was trained as a chemical engineer! I couldn't be a life coach. That was crazy.

And yet, I couldn't not do it, because I kept asking myself that simple question: "Why doesn't everybody know about this stuff?"

My business grew quickly. I had growing pains, of course, but I'd already done so much work to get to this point. More, I knew how to select containers of support that would not just help me grow my business but also reveal my deepest Truths and transform my own inner barriers to business success.

Before long, I was able to consistently bring in clients at a very high level even though I was still "new" in business. At the same time, many of the coaches around me were struggling to sell their work. Their business gurus would tell them, "Just keep selling." But under all the flashy marketing and perfect brand photos, there was a deep fear ... a fear that they couldn't deliver on the transformation they were promising to their clients.

Now, as a new coach, I had all sorts of fears. I wondered, Will anyone ever listen to me? How can I ask for money for this? What if people don't like me?

But I was on fire for transformation. I knew that, once someone said yes to working with me and stepped into my container, they would see their Truth, and their life would never be the same.

I had no idea that the way I viewed my transformational work was unique to me. I figured that, if someone had received the same type of training I had, they must be doing the same things I was. I didn't realize that I had a special magic in the world of transformation—and that I needed to be talking about it!

(Truth time: even after training transformational retreat leaders for years, teaching them the contents of this book and watching it change them, and developing a whole series on owning your magic, I still feel shy to write this.)

I'd like to say that I figured this out after hiring a few coaches who talked about transformation but didn't really know how deliver it. Or after attending countless mastermind retreats with other business owners who were far more interested in finding email subject lines to tug at their prospects' heartstrings than in helping their newly acquired clients to heal their hearts. Or after coaching client after client who worried that, even after extensive training in their unique modality, they had no idea how to actually deliver their work.

But no. None of that brought it home for me.

It wasn't until I began expanding my business by hiring associate coaches to my team that I finally recognized that not everybody was seeing transformation the way I did. Not everyone saw the energy patterns that people were bringing to their work and knew that one shift would make all the difference. Not even people who had been through the Fishbowl or other similar trainings consistently understood when and how to hold space for Truth and the freedom it could bring. And, most importantly, people did not seem to have a firm grasp on a structure for approaching energy patterns within their work.

There is a predictable way to uncover truth and shift the energy field with your clients. No matter what modality, business model, or delivery mechanism you're using, you can deliver transformation consistently.

Every. Single. Time.

For years, I'd been able to see how my clients could design their retreats around predictable transformation. I could see how their business model was or wasn't supporting the structure needed to facilitate transformation and get paid for it.

But it wasn't until I began having conversations with my team—who were working with my clients, with a goal of delivering my promised outcomes—that I really saw the gap. They were fabulous and talented, but they weren't holding a firm container to help our clients shift their energy fields in the way I was. They weren't putting the revelation and integration of our clients' personal Truth at the center of the experience. They didn't know to do it. I hadn't told them. I had just assumed everyone knew what I knew.

This blew my mind.

I began to look back at all the coaches and consultants I'd worked with in my own journey. Several of them didn't know how to hold a transformational container, either. They would ask during each call what I wanted to work on, and allow me, whether I was in my ego—what we'll come to call Default Energy—or I was in my aligned Sourced Energy, to run the show. They didn't know how to create a firm container of support. And when I had a breakthrough—when another piece of my Truth was revealed—they didn't always understand how to hold me in that space until I could integrate that new, higher-level energy. I always got great results, not just because I was coachable, but because I brought my own knowledge of how transformation works to the table. I was certain I would have a transformational experience with my coaches because I knew how to create one for myself. (And if I was working with a coach who was masterful at this, the experience was even more profound and potent.)

STRUCTURE AND FLOW

It is my assumption that you are coming to this book with intuitive transformational gifts. It's also likely that you have had various trainings and life experiences in this area. In other words, you are magical!

My intention in this book is not for you to change anything about your unique approach to your work. In fact, that would be counterproductive! Instead, I want to provide a framework for creating transformation that will allow you to lean even further into your already-present magic and bring forth the kernels of field-shifting Truth that are ready to be revealed to you and your clients. Because you can trust this structure to hold you and your clients through whatever arises, you will be able to show up even more fully in your intuitive gifts.

This structure, which I call "The Anatomy of a Transformation," is the heart of this book. It's a strong container which uses masculine energy to create solidity, boundaries, and support. Truth—our personal, intuitive, innate knowing—is the heart of this container. Later in this book, I'll explain in greater depth the role Truth plays in transformation. For now, understand that when you bring someone into a transformational space, Truth is what you are inviting.

When you lean into the firm container of The Anatomy of a Transformation, you will be able to bring more feminine energy (aka, freedom and flow) to your work and leadership. You will be able to access your powerful intuitive gifts to create a safe space for your clients to Release their old ways of being, Receive their personal Truth, and Rise into a new, transformed energy.

This balance between masculine structure and feminine flow is key when it comes to creating transformation.

Please note that, when I speak about "masculine" or "feminine" here, I am referring to energies, not genders. And while I don't teach about these polarities specifically in this book, know that they are present, as they are in all things. As a gay woman, female engineer, and student of divine flow in all things, I promise that the ability to harness both energies is priceless. It doesn't matter whether you are in a male or female body, or identify as both or neither. When you put a structure (masculine) in place to support the container of your work, you will be able to bring a more nurturing, fun, and playful (feminine) approach to your delivery.

Speaking of gender: While I myself go by the pronouns she/her, I salute those who are choosing gender-neutral pronouns, providing even more space for our species to flow between masculine and feminine qualities. You may notice that, throughout this book, I have opted to use the pronoun "they" when talking about a hypothetical client or client situation. (Of course, when I include stories about actual client experiences, I always honor their chosen pronouns.) While this may not be grammatically correct in the old-school way (which would require using "he" or "he or she" for nonspecific references), I am committed to inclusivity. It's my wish that this adjustment flows clearly for you.

Here's what else you can expect as you move through this book.

In Part I, we'll discuss what it means to Shift the Field, and how this potent transformation of energy aligns your clients perfectly with the outcomes they seek. We'll explore what it means to approach your business with a "Transformation First" mindset—including how you can recognize and lean into Sourced Experiences in your own life, even when shit is hitting the fan—and the missing piece that keeps so many coaches and businesses from actually delivering the transformation they promise.

In Part II, I'll introduce The Anatomy of a Transformation, my signature approach to creating life-changing client results. This process was developed over years of leading my own transformational programs as a business coach, and eventually launching my own multi-six-figure business building formula called Retreat and Grow Rich. The Anatomy of a Transformation is a three-stage approach designed to support you and your clients as you move together, with divine guidance, through the transformational process. Its three key steps—Commitment, The Sourced Experience™, and Integration—bring your clients' Truth to center stage. This spotlighting of Truth (as opposed to strategy or process) reliably creates transformation whether you're working with high-level clients one-on-one, leading a group program or mastermind, or hosting a transformational retreat.

In Part III, we'll take what you've learned about transformation and apply it to the structures in your business. We'll explore your magical intuitive gifts, and why you may wish to rethink what (and how) you're selling in your business! We'll look at your business model and align your offers with The Anatomy of a Transformation to create a more streamlined client experience and lasting results. Finally, I'll share some key tips and resources (including how to contact and work with me) to help you create Shift the Field experiences within your coaching programs, either in person or virtually.

I haven't got quantitative scientific research to back up my claims about transformation in this book (although I'm absolutely open to finding a way to create it!). However, my decades of personal experience, coupled with the experiences of thousands of transformed clients, serve as qualitative data to support my conclusions.

That said, I don't expect you to simply take my word for it! Throughout this book, I'll share my own stories and those of my clients to illustrate the concepts I'm sharing. Open your heart, and trust what resonates. Leave the rest.

My wish for you as you engage with this work is that you are affirmed in what you know and how you already work—and that you also experience that singular click, that a-ha moment, that allows you to Shift the Field in your own life and work. Maybe this book will lead you to your own "punch in the gut" moment of realization. Maybe it will simply offer a gentle invitation to lean into the subtler energies of the work you're already doing. Either way, my goal is to empower you to instantly create exponential results for yourself and your clients.

Let the Shift begin!

PART I

A COMMITMENT TO TRANSFORMATION

CHAPTER ONE
SHIFT THE FIELD

"*I*n theory, I should be feeling great. I did what I set out to do by transitioning my business, but it just feels … off. If I don't sort this out, I don't know what I'll do instead. I'm unemployable at this point, yet I can't keep going like this."

Those were the first words Brittany shared with the group on day one of our transformational retreat. I knew exactly how she was feeling.

Like so many healers, coaches, consultants, and service-based entrepreneurs, Brittany was tired. She was juggling so many balls as a business owner, and as a service provider who was committed to the best for her clients, she was often over-giving. In the evenings, when she wanted to simply be present for her partner, she was either on the couch with her laptop writing blog posts or thinking about a client situation she didn't know how to resolve. She loved her work on the whole, but in the big picture it wasn't working.

On the outside, Brittany was super successful. She had previously built a thriving therapy practice. She has a master's degree, several certifications in alternative therapies, and a large network of referral sources. She was curious and resourceful, always looking for the best approach to support her clients.

It was this drive that led her to transition out of her therapy practice and into more transformational work as a coach. She didn't want to "diagnose" her clients anymore. She wanted to help awesome humans like herself live a more empowered life.

Brittany was just over a year into her coaching work when she registered for our Sourced Experience™. At that point, she had successfully stopped seeing clients as a therapist; she had doubled her pricing, no longer took any insurance, and required all new clients to sign up for a minimum of three months of coaching. She let go of her physical office and was conducting all sessions by phone. Fully half of her clients made the shift to the new model and loved it, and without insurance and rent costs, she was making significantly more money.

Brittany had also recently begun offering transformational workshops to groups of her clients, knowing that she could help them go deeper this way. Her clients were excited to come to the workshops.

As she had said, in theory she should have been feeling great. But she wasn't.

She thought she would be able to get better results with clients without the shackles of insurance forms and diagnoses. And sometimes it seemed like she was, because she felt free to ask better questions and go off script. But then a client would take a step back, or a workshop participant would show a lot of resistance, and Brittany instantly felt defeated. Because clients were paying her more, she felt more responsible than ever for making them happy. And even though she was making more than last year, Brittany saw other coaches around her earning far more than she was, with a fraction of her qualifications! More, after nine months in a business mastermind and following her coach's formula, she was doing more to attract new clients, but getting little in the way of results. Deep down, Brittany didn't really want more clients, because more clients meant more work, more stress, and more time spent on her business. Being in constant hustle mode made her feel less effective in her client work, not more.

Something had to change.

"I know my clients love me," Brittany stated. "For many, I'm their inspiration and sense of stability, and I love that. But I can't keep this up. I'm just so worried that I'll let them down."

"I hear you," I said. "I've been there, and there is a practical solution. But before you can change your business, you need to find out where this is all coming from. This isn't just about strategy, Brittany, it's about Energy."

Over the course of the retreat, I got to know more about Brittany. Her mother had raised her and her two siblings virtually alone. Her father traveled for work as a truck driver for long stretches, and when he was home he was more interested in drinking than his children. His drinking, and the fact that he wanted things to be exactly how he wanted them, led to terrible fights between her parents.

With her mother working long hours, Brittany, as the oldest child, began taking on responsibility for her siblings. She would notice when the laundry needed to be done and take care of it, and she could tell when her mom was too tired to ask about homework or tuck them into bed. She even reminded her mom when the rent was due.

When Dad was home, Brittany was sure to keep things extra orderly and smooth in an attempt to prevent him from taking issue with her mother. And while it didn't always work, Brittany knew that he was pleased with her at least—her work ethic and commitment to the family shone through. Her dad criticized her younger siblings for being lazy or causing trouble, but she knew she would never be faulted or hurt as long as she played this vital role. She was the reason the household ran—even if her mom didn't know it. She was the quietly responsible one, and it kept her safe.

What Brittany came to learn on our retreat was that she was running her business the same way she'd run her household—from a position of fear. She was "quietly responsible," caretaking and managing her clients' issues the same way she'd been caretaking her mom, her siblings, and her dad. But she had never been able to change him—and she wasn't helping her clients change either.

This pattern was revealed early on in our retreat during an experiential exercise. Each randomly selected team was to reach a specific outcome within a set period of time, and the winning team would be rewarded. Achieving the goal required the team to agree upon and execute a strategy efficiently, and without missing any details.

As luck would have it (though it's never luck!), Brittany ended up with the perfect team for her. It was as if her team was made up of the same people that she'd had in her family! They were also the same people that were her roommates in college, and the colleagues in the therapy practice where she worked before going out on her own. In other words, she found herself having the same familiar experience that had been repeating throughout her whole life.

In particular, one of her teammates had quite a dominant personality, and deemed himself the one in charge, just like Brittany's father. There was the woman with her head in the clouds, reminiscent of her mother. Her other two team members seemed … just okay. In response, Brittany found herself rallying the less dominant members of the team to get it together and do the exercise right. She didn't need to win, but she sure as hell wasn't going to lose.

Throughout the exercise she was subconsciously seeking the approval of the "man in charge." That same feeling she'd experienced throughout most of her childhood was welling up in her stomach, but she barely noticed it; it was just "the water she swam in." But she sure was frustrated. Trying to get it all done and keep everyone on the team happy was extremely stressful!

Brittany's result was perfect, just as designed, but not because her team won (they didn't). Because as we debriefed the exercise, she discovered that this way of being was actually the way she was showing up in all the areas of her life: taking responsibility, making sure everyone on the team was okay, diminishing her contribution publicly so the self-appointed leader still felt like he was in charge, while secretly knowing that she did it all! The purpose of the experience was to reveal to participants the way of being they default to in a challenging situation, which would mirror the way they are being that had been creating their current business challenge.

As Brittany began to explore this idea, she could see exactly how the pattern that revealed itself in the exercise was also showing up in her business.

She could see that she was working hard to figure out how to do it all, how to make her clients happy, how to please the coach who was giving her advice on how to run her business (aka, the "man in charge"), and make time for her home life. But what was really hard to see and admit to herself was how, ever so subtly, she saw her clients as incapable of managing their own lives.

Brittany was horrified to see this truth. But it wasn't her fault. In her situation growing up, it really did seem that if she didn't take care of things, no one else would or could. She'd done this so often, it had become a natural approach to life, and necessary for her own survival. If she didn't take responsibility for things, it meant Mom and Dad were sure to fight, and the terror of that had been more than she could stand.

While she was led to coaching because she wanted to empower her clients, she suddenly realized that she had a filter for them—for everyone really—that had her seeing all the places they "needed help," rather than seeing their power.

She could now see, with the support of my guidance, that it hadn't actually been true that it was her job to take care of things for her family. She was just a kid. But it made perfect sense that it had felt that way, and that she'd created this pattern.

As soon as Brittany could see that she'd been showing up this way (her team went out on a limb to express how they'd felt diminished as she quietly took control of the exercise), she knew she was ready to let this pattern go.

As she began to explore what that might look and feel like, she realized something else.

While in some ways Brittany felt totally self-important—my clients need me, I have to get this done—she also felt very hidden.

When she handled things for her parents, she did so quietly. She never took credit; it was simply expected. As she watched the coaches in her new industry "put themselves out there" and promote their work, giving clear opinions and getting noticed, Brittany felt terrified.

Staying focused on her clients and what they needed from her, giving them extra sessions, offering workshops for free, emailing them resources after hours ... suddenly Brittany could realize how nicely this old pattern kept her safe in another way. Not only would her clients love and approve of her, but as long as she was busy with that, she didn't have to formulate her point of view, or do the things she knew she needed to do to get visible, bring in more clients, and move beyond her financial set point.

The decision Brittany had made as a middle schooler was still subtly controlling her life. This pattern had allowed her to survive in a household that wasn't set up to nurture her success—but she'd trapped herself in a dynamic of needing to be responsible and in control of everything to stay safe, while at the same time flying under the radar and making everyone else feel like they were doing it on their own. Even becoming a therapist had been part of the pattern: a built-in group of people who "needed" her, and a strict set of rules to which she was legally bound.

As she got present to it, Brittany could even feel the pattern in her body; it showed up as tension in her shoulders from carrying those burdens, and a concavity in her chest from her efforts to stay hidden.

When she began to see and work with this old energy pattern (as I will teach you to do with your own clients in this book), she felt it release from her physical and emotional bodies. She seemed to stand a full foot taller. Her fellow retreat-goers described her as "glowing," or "lit up." On the last day of the retreat, she put on a bright purple dress.

"I had no idea at the time why I packed this," she said. "But now I do. It's time for me to be seen."

This new Brittany was not responsible for everyone. She didn't try to do it all or avoid upsetting people by keeping the peace. She was ready to remove the burden of that responsibility from her life and her work. She was ready to be more free, vibrant, and connected—in other words, to be more of who she truly was.

Most of all, she was ready to support her clients in a way that would allow them to do the same.

But as she packed her things to head for home, she also noticed a small feeling of fear in the pit of her stomach. What would it actually take to follow through on this? What would her partner think of her choices? Of her new energy? When she worried about this, she felt her shoulders hunch forward in that familiar "hiding" position. Each time she noticed this, she pulled her shoulders back, stood tall, and continued to experience herself anew.

While Brittany traveled home, she found it was a whole new experience. People seemed to respond to her differently—when ordering her coffee at the airport, when boarding the plane. She had the most delightful conversation with her seatmate, who was clearly grateful to meet her! No one wanted anything from her, no one overlooked her; she was important and expressive. This feeling was wonderful.

She'd spoken to her partner by phone before returning home, so he was prepared for a change. He was supportive at first. He told her how happy he was for her, and carried in her bags with delight.

The next morning, however, when the new Brittany decided to have a quick coffee and head out to the gym without preparing breakfast and taking care of things around the house first, he didn't much like this change. Unconsciously, he began piling up work for Brittany—laundry here, dishes there—because he was committed to Brittany staying the same. While he really did want her to be happy, it was clear that the old version of her had been working for him quite nicely.

When she returned to her business, Brittany found that her clients seemed to need her more than ever. While her life had totally transformed on the inside, no one there had gotten the memo! Suddenly, there was that old, heavy feeling in her body—but this time, she recognized it as her Default Energy.

TWO TYPES OF ENERGY

In this book we will come to understand two types of energy: Default Energy and Sourced Energy. Our energy creates a field around us, and that field determines the playing field for our life.

When Brittany arrived on retreat, she was in her Default Energy, diminishing both herself and those she "needed" to help, quietly taking responsibility and control in a way that made her feel indispensable. But she didn't know this about herself; she simply was the way she was, and life was the way it was, and there was nothing unusual to her about how events unfolded. It was her exhaustion, not her awareness of her Default Energy, that brought her to my Sourced Experience retreat. Were it not for the transformational intention of the retreat, she would have left with a renewed energy but no long-term solutions.

Default Energy is the energy field we developed in response to our experiences in life, and it serves as an overarching survival, or success, strategy. Our Default Energy is like the familiar water we swim in. We may not be getting the results we want, but they are results we are accustomed to. Default Energy limits what is available to us.

Brittany left the retreat in a whole new energy, or "vibe" if you will—free, vibrant, and connected. You can just feel the difference, can't you? As Brittany closed out her retreat and traveled home, she experienced life through this field, and she noticed a distinct difference in how the world responded to her. She was drawn to different experiences, and, in turn, they were drawn to her.

Brittany came to our retreat in Default Energy, but she left in Sourced Energy—and opened the door to a whole new way of being in the world.

Sourced Energy is aligned with who we truly are at a soul level, and is alive for us. It expands what it is possible for us to experience in life. It quite literally creates a different reality.

In essence, it shifts the playing field of life.

But it does not happen by accident.

SHIFTING THE FIELD

Shifting the Field is my way of referring to the energetic up-grade we can make any time our results aren't bringing us the experience we desire. It's a conscious shift from Default Energy to Sourced Energy. This shift is at the heart of the process of transformation.

If you're reading this book, the idea of transformation is most likely not new to you. You've probably experienced some form of transformation in your own life; this is likely what draws you to become a catalyst for this type of foundational shift in your clients' lives as well.

To create common ground here, let's start by defining some initial terminology.

- **Transformation:** A new awareness that results in a perma-nent shift in how we show up and interact with life, and therefore in the results we receive. This change shifts our *energy field*.

- **Energy:** The vibrational state of our cells. Our energy is represented by our *way of being* (*beingness*) in the world. Our thoughts and feelings work together to create our en-ergy state as a vibrational frequency in the cells of our body and the field around our body. Our energy interacts with the outside world to create our reality. When we shift our energy (transform), we shift our reality.

- **The Field:** Merriam-Webster defines "field" as "a region or space in which a given effect exists; or, a complex of forces that serve as causative agents in human behavior." When I speak about "Shifting the Field," I am referring to a shift in one's energy field that becomes a causative agent for a shift in the behavior of the humans around us!

- **Source:** Source is the grand energy field of the divine, which exists all around us and within us, and which carries an infinite wisdom. For me this is a spiritual energy that I also refer to as God, Spirit, or the Universe. Merriam-Webster defines the word "source" *as a generative force, cause, or point of origin.* This applies to how I hold the concept of Source here as well. The energy of Source is a generative force, the point of origin from which we came. I don't personally ascribe to a specific religion, but I can see that most major religions seek to define this same spiritual energy and make it accessible.

- **Sourced:** Literally, "of Source." Living from Sourced Energy demonstrates a commitment to hearing the wisdom of Source working with and through you for the greatest good, and for your highest expression. Also, a Sourced decision or action is one which has come from your personal sense of alignment with your own inner knowing, as opposed to external influences. Sourced decisions are made from Sourced Energy, not Default Energy. The process of Shifting the Field from Default to Sourced Energy is what we will be covering in this book.

If you are a coach, consultant, healer, teacher, trainer, or service provider committed to creating *true transformation* for your clients (as opposed to just progress), this book is for you. You're no longer satisfied with clients bumping up against the same problems or blocks. You no longer want to teach techniques or strategies that clients don't implement. You no longer want to carry the weight of responsibility for others' outcomes.

Instead, you want to go deeper with clients, and help them to create a permanent shift in how they play the game of life. You want to facilitate real change for those you serve, whether individually or in groups. And you want to be confident that you can accomplish this over and over, using your unique magic and gifts, for anyone who is ready for that level of transformation.

WHAT ARE YOU AVAILABLE FOR?

Everything we observe is coming in through the filter of *our own energy field.*

Two people can witness the same scene unfold on the street and reach completely different conclusions. Two people can come to the same retreat and have totally different experiences. Two people can have totally different takeaways from the same conversation. This is because of the *energy* through which they are filtering their experience.

Your energy field is putting a signal out to the world, to all the possible people and experiences you could choose to interact with. Your field signals to the world—and your clients— what you are *available for.*

If you are reading this book, this is likely not a new concept for you. You may have studied the Law of Attraction, read Wayne Dyer's books, or listened to Abraham Hicks. But you are about to explore this in a whole new way: as a business owner, service provider, and facilitator of transformation for others.

This is incredibly important because in order to create the kind of results we want for our clients, we have to be available for those results, too. If we want to help others shift into Sourced Energy, we have to be willing to become Sourced ourselves.

When Brittany was living in Default Energy, she always saw opportunities to take on projects that would let her fly under the radar while at the same time being indispensable to someone. When her field said, "Go ahead and leave that with me, I can take care of it," that is exactly what people did in response. They left her with their emotional baggage, their to-do lists, and the burden of their transformation. She didn't need to say it directly; her energy told people that she was available for taking responsibility for whatever came her way if it would keep the peace!

Even in an identical business model, someone with a different energy would not have had that same experience. And, as I'll share in upcoming chapters, Brittany's experience—and, in fact, her entire business model—changed once she began to show up consistently in her Sourced Energy.

As service providers, the quality of our energy field determines not only what we experience in life, but also what our clients experience with us. And so, in order to create the kinds of Sourced transformations we desire for those we serve, we have to be willing to become Sourced ourselves.

As you read this book, you'll notice that I have created not only a pathway for you to Shift the Field for your clients, but also to do it for yourself. This way, both you and they can be available for life-changing results.

THE PURPOSE OF IT ALL

What if the purpose of life—mine and yours—was simply to become more of who we came here to be as unique souls?

We were born to express a unique flavor of Source. I call this your "Sourced Expression." Our individual divine curriculum is designed to help us see our Default Energy patterns and use them to help us unleash more Sourced Energy in our life.

What if everything you've experienced was exactly how you were meant to discover who you came here to be? Your life is one big invitation to grow into a new, expanded, Sourced Energy—one that allows you to experience the Truth of who you are more fully. And that includes your business.

We are conditioned in more ways than we can count to judge that Y is better than X, and that we should be A and not B. As someone who wants to facilitate change and growth for others, this is doubly true. You may be inundated with techniques, strategies, and to-dos around your own business and your clients' results. Like Brittany, you may feel that you're not doing enough, or that you just need to learn a new system or modality to help your clients get the results they're craving.

Only *you*, in connection with Source, hold your personal Truth about who you came here to be and how you came here to serve. You will find that Truth not through other people's strategies and systems, but through the ongoing experience and practice of Shifting the Field.

This book isn't about teaching you my personal way of facilitating transformation. It's about helping you find and apply your unique gifts *within a proven transformational framework*, and then unleash them as the fully-Sourced version of yourself.

To be Sourced is to live with the knowing that your divine purpose is to become a greater expression of Source energy in this world for the benefit of all. That means being willing to clearly see who you came here to be—and release everything that is not aligned with that, over and over again.

Throughout this book, I will show you how to work with all of the experiences in your clients' lives to create more alignment. I'll teach you about the three big stages in The Anatomy of a Transformation, and how they work in practice. I'll also guide you through the three unique steps within the core of the Anatomy (which I call The Sourced Experience) and how to hold space for your clients at each specific step.

I will share tools and perspectives that support you in guiding your clients to discover their divine purpose (being more of who they came here to be), working within The Anatomy of a Transformation. We'll also explore when and how to move your clients to the next stage in their journey in your role as coach, facilitator, or retreat leader.

However, I want you to view all of this through the lens of your own unique gifts. Again, this is a framework, not an instruction manual. There is room for all of your Sourced decisions, talents, gifts, and expression within it.

When Brittany shifted her field, she was able to relax the grip she had on her clients' results and hold the whole experience of her business more lightly. But the change was bigger than that. She became more ... Brittany.

Under her quietly responsible cloak was a vibrant woman who had loads of clear opinions on what worked. When she stopped worrying about everyone else and focused instead on the new energy of *free, vibrant, and connected,* Brittany could suddenly see her unique way of approaching her business. She had to *be* that energy so that her clients would sense that she was no longer available for caretaking them.

This started in small ways—like an "I'll get back to you on Monday" message when a client reached out on the weekend and also charging for her previously complimentary workshops. She promptly and light-heartedly ended a call early when a client hadn't completed the action they had committed to. It didn't take long before her new energy permeated these relationships, and the clients were showing up differently of their own accord. By shifting her field, Brittany had shifted theirs, too!

The situation with her husband felt trickier. After all, she had committed to him for life, not just a three-month engagement. And while she could tell that he found her new energy attractive, she also knew he was irritated with her change in focus. She ignored it at first, doing her best to keep up with all of her typical at-home tasks and appear the same. But when she watched the energy with her clients shift before her eyes, she knew she could "go there" with her husband, too.

She asked him to share what he had noticed was different about her, and how he felt about it. She stayed open as he revealed what he liked, and what he didn't. She then began to share what her new energy meant to her, and how she'd like their relationship to be to support her in being free, vibrant, and connected. "Since we are so connected, my energy affects you, too," she told him. "So I'm committing to be my best self—not just for me, but for you, and for us."

How could he resist this idea? Together, they brainstormed ways he could take on more of the "doing" at home, so she had more space to "be."

And speaking of connected, when Brittany stopped being so in the weeds with her to-do lists, she could now see that one of her greatest strengths was connection! This was an innate gift for her, but she'd pushed it down in her Default Energy, when it had felt like every new relationship was based on someone needing something from her. Now that she was free to shine vibrantly and connect authentically, she realized that nearly everyone she met thought she was amazing and wanted to support her. She built a network of strategic referral partners, and soon her calendar was filling up with clients who were aligned with her unique approach, totally committed to their own transformation, and willing to invest at a high level.

This happened first and foremost because Brittany Shifted the Field.

Undergoing her own transformation empowered Brittany to align with the transformation she wanted to create for others. She learned, and was now prepared to work within, an experiential framework that could consistently produce life-changing results—the same framework you are about to learn in this book.

Before we get into the details, though, let's get anchored into what it is to be a service provider who actually leads with transformation, and who begins *all* client engagements by Shifting the Field.

CHAPTER TWO
TRANSFORMATION FIRST

*K*risty knew it was time to make some major changes in her business, but she just couldn't seem to pull the trigger.

When we hopped on a call to explore whether I would be the right coach to help her, I learned that Kristy was no stranger to career or professional changes, or the courage it took to put herself out there. She had worked her way up within her former company from skilled assistant to office manager before leaving to start her own consulting business. Now, her business was thriving, earning over a half million dollars in annual revenue—more money than she'd ever dreamed possible. She had far surpassed anyone's expectations for her new venture, including her own.

Normally, when she knew she wanted something, she could push herself to go for it, even when she was afraid—but this time, it was different. She'd taken all kinds of courses and worked with other coaches on her mindset and business strategy, but for some reason she couldn't talk herself into moving forward toward her latest goal. Something else was going on, and so she'd reached out to me for help to move past this stuck point.

Kristy's business provided systems and training for business professionals in a niche industry. Her clients loved her, and they got results. She'd done an excellent job of following the advice of various business experts: she had chosen a specific niche, developed high-end consulting packages, and hired support staff to help deliver the work. In theory, she should have been happy.

However, a few things about this structure weren't working for her.

First, she was traveling to her clients to help them implement their systems. At first it was super fun to travel and get paid, and she was great at playing investigator in her client's offices. But eventually, the "road warrior" life grew tiresome. She wanted to be more present for the children in her life, rather than just trying to fit in quality time between business trips. She'd discovered that all of her clients needed one of three things: technical systems, customer service training, or new product education. There had to be a more effective way to deliver this!

Second, Kristy wanted to pay herself more and work less. Even though she had hired support staff, she still had to direct a lot of what was happening. While it had seemed like the right thing at the time to move beyond one-to-one services, she was actually working more than she had before she'd hired people, and now she had to share the proceeds. This equation wasn't serving her.

Third, Kristy had discovered something as she gained more experience working with clients: while she regularly helped them double their revenue and make their offices more efficient, the clients themselves were not any happier! She was helping them get the results they thought they wanted, but in the end, they were not getting the results they truly needed. This gap in her clients' happiness kept her up at night more than anything.

Through her own work as a business owner, she had discovered that building a business around what she wanted (instead of what she thought the business needed), and consistently working with her own mindset, was the key to being happier. *This* was the stuff she wanted to share with her clients—but they were paying her to implement systems and train staff, not help them be happy!

Being the smart, adaptable leader that she is, Kristy decided to test her ideas for what she really wanted to offer her clients to help them make more money *and* be happier. She began offering live retreats. Her goals were to disseminate information to groups in order to avoid travelling to individual offices (or sending one of her support staff there), and to encourage attendees to explore what actually made them happy by removing the demands of their day-to-day businesses.

Her clients immediately loved these retreats, and she loved doing them.

But here was the problem: she was doing them for *free*!

And because they required resources to put together and host, she was actually *making less money* because she was doing retreats!

This wasn't a problem for her at first. She considered it market research, a way to test her ideas. But by the time she got on our call, she'd been "testing" for two years. but she still hadn't started charging for this valuable work. She had a secret vision for a business based entirely on live retreats and leveraged training programs, but for some reason couldn't bring herself to pull the trigger.

She had logical questions, like, "Will this really work?" "Will my clients pay as much to work with me in this new way?" and "Can I trust myself to deliver?" But she'd dealt with thoughts like these before and had moved through them. This time, there was more to the situation, and she knew it.

By the time we were halfway through our initial conversation, I knew it, too.

Let me be clear: I had no idea what the "more" was, or what changes she would need to make to her business to make this work. I simply knew that there was something in her way, and that my process for creating transformation would help her shift it.

When I asked her to invest with me, she cried, because she'd already invested tens of thousands of dollars with other coaches to try to solve this problem. This time, she would invest even more (working privately with me is a high-level investment), but she knew intuitively that this time she *would* get the results she was craving. She grieved the money and time she'd already spent, but also how long she'd been living in fear—and she cried with joy because she was finally saying yes to herself.

By the end of our year together, Kristy made the changes to her programs that she'd envisioned for so long—and she did it *without losing a single dollar of revenue.*

She swapped out office visits to her clients for in-person leadership retreats. She released one team member and redesigned her programs so that work with an on-site team member was available at an additional fee (meaning it was no longer cutting into her personal pay).

Her clients who wanted to be truly *happy* while making more money stayed with her, paying the same amount for a more leveraged offering. Those who didn't want to do the inner leadership work moved on, but new clients immediately came in to fill their spots. Thus, Kristy was able to maintain the same cash flow with less of her time.

What had she been waiting for? What had been stopping her? And how did I help her to shift her energy field in order to make the changes necessary for her to achieve her goals?

In this chapter we'll explore what I call The Anatomy of a Transformation, and why you don't actually have to understand what your clients need to shift in order to know that your programs will work for them. You'll learn that transformation has a predictable rhythm, and that when you master this flow you can easily use the Anatomy to Shift the Field.

I could have never predicted what would unfold for Kristy, but I *knew* it would unfold, which is why I felt confident asking her to invest in an outcome without knowing anything about her true problem.

Many service providers get this wrong. They either try to solve the problem before they've collected payment (detailed proposals, anyone?), or they assume that everyone who comes to them has the same problem to solve. Both approaches lead with logic rather than Sourced Energy. And neither leave room for the magical process of true transformation—the process of Shifting the Field.

WHY TRANSFORMATION COMES FIRST

When we think about changing something in our lives—creating a new business, achieving a goal, losing weight, finding a partner, etc.—what we really want is to experience a new *energy*. If we don't Shift the Field first, we can cross all the right things off our to-do lists but end up feeling just as unfulfilled as when we started.

In working with your clients, if you don't lead with transformation, you'll find yourself helping them to create something that is technically "right." But there's a high likelihood that they will create that result from the exact same energy they are trying to get away from. What follows is a "Groundhog Day" experience of a life on repeat.

When I left my corporate career for the first time to become a teacher, I expected everything to be different. After all, engineering and teaching high school math had virtually nothing in common—except the math.

I changed my circumstance, but I hadn't Shifted the Field. And so, I found I had many of the same complaints in my new career as I'd had in the old one! For example, I was teaching in an amazing school, yet I perceived that my fellow teachers weren't doing enough to help the students. This was exactly the same as how I'd felt when I thought my engineering colleagues could have done more to move our projects forward. I took on the weight and burden of doing more in both places. That was all me; I'd brought that with me.

Luckily, I found a retreat that began teaching me the principles of transformation, and ultimately changed my life. (I share more about my own transformation in my first book, *Retreat and Grow Rich.*)

Would I still be where I am if I'd learned how to Shift the Field before making that career change? I like to think so; Source has a way of guiding us to where we need to be. But I can guarantee I would have had a better experience as a teacher!

We can bring Sourced Energy to any life path. No matter who your clients are, or what changes they are making, leading with transformation will help them reach their goals faster, more predictably, and more powerfully.

Don't be afraid to focus on energy first. Don't be afraid to take a stand for your client's transformation. Don't be afraid to speak your Truth, and to trust where your intuition guides you as a coach and leader (as you'll discover in Part II, Truth is the pivot point for Shifting the Field!) Sourced Energy is Truth energy. When you hold the space for your client's transformation—even if you're not clear what that transformation will entail—you are holding space for your client's Truth. And when you can coach your client into operating from a Sourced Energy field, they will be creating the most truthful, aligned life they can possibly live.

So many service providers are so focused on "doing." We offer "*done* for you" and "*done* with you" services. We teach clients what to *do* and hold them accountable to getting it *done*. But so many of us get scared when it comes to helping clients actually *be* different.

When we help someone Shift the Field, the new way of being that results is natural and inspiring. But getting someone across that threshold requires boldness, clarity, and a willingness on your part to support the real work that needs to be done as it reveals itself.

Your clients want this from you. Your soul wants it, too.

YOUR CLIENTS *WANT* TRANSFORMATION FIRST

Whether they know it or not—and whether *you* know it or not—your clients actually want transformation first.

When I was coming up in the coaching world, I was repeatedly spoon-fed this mantra: "*Sell them what they want. Give them what they need.*"

Initially I bought this idea hook, line, and sinker. After all, the people who were teaching me were *way* more successful than I was. And there was logic to the idea that people want to buy a specific outcome. That's basic marketing.

For your client, choosing transformation means choosing to look at truths about themselves that they haven't previously seen. This is inherently intimidating. It makes sense that other coaches might want to sneak it in the back door.

But after ten years of selling transformation, I've discovered a few things.

First, when someone doesn't want transformation, you can't drag them into it. So, you might as well be upfront about what working with you requires. This doesn't mean sharing all of *how* you work, or even *what* they will transform. However, they do need to know that they will transform, that you will provide a safe space to help them do it, and that reaching their desired outcome will be worth moving through that discomfort.

Second, your clients are aware that what's blocking them is hidden from their view in some way. If they could see what needed to shift, they would have already addressed it. When you let them see that you understand this, they will hear the truth in your reflection.

Third, the old "sell them what they want, give them what they need" approach is highly disempowering. It implies that your clients don't know—or worse, aren't capable of knowing—what they need. This is in direct conflict with the premise of coaching, and the idea of living Sourced, because transformation always comes from within the client and not from the coach.

Fourth, the market for transformation is becoming more sophisticated. People are more discerning about who they hire for this work and are willing to invest substantial time and money when they know it will help them create real change. I personally have paid hundreds of thousands of dollars for my own transformation—far more than I have for external strategies and formulas—and I've received many times that amount in revenue as a result.

The clients who seek you out for your commitment to transformation are heroes. They know they must adventure deep into their own truth to reach their desires, and they know that regardless of what you teach them, it's up to them to change if they want lasting results. What they want isn't for you to have all the answers, but for you to hold them in the highest light as they go into their darkest depths and emerge again in powerful alignment.

TRANSFORMATION IS PREDICTABLE

Since you picked up this book, it's likely that you have—or are learning that you have—a plethora of intuitive and healing gifts. This is what I call your "magic."

Some of these gifts you came by naturally—like the intuition you were forced to hone to stay safe in your household growing up, or the naturally open emotional center that allows you to feel and mirror back other people's feelings, or the solid sense of self that allows people to feel more comfortable being themselves in your presence.

Other gifts have been developed through training and experience, like your skill with certain coaching approaches or modalities.

It's possible that you haven't claimed the moniker of "healer" yet. That's totally okay. I was healing for years before I recognized myself in the word. Today, I know all the healing I do is simply facilitating awareness in others so that they can heal themselves.

Whatever your gifts, and regardless of the modalities you use to deliver those gifts, you can be a catalyst for transformation. As you deepen your understanding of the mechanism of transformation, you will find new and creative ways to apply it to your specific approach.

It's important to know that delivering transformation to your clients is not about doing things in one specific way all the time. (That would be incredibly boring!) However, transformation is, itself, predictable. You simply need to understand how it works so you can hold the intentional space your clients need to get out of their own way and come into energetic harmony with the results they desire.

When Kristy first came to me, she wasn't earning money from her transformational retreats because she wasn't yet in energetic harmony with doing so. Before she could put any of the strategies she learned with me to work—like how to structure her offers, what to charge, and how to talk about her programs—she needed to transform her old, default energies. I knew this would happen, even if I didn't know the details yet, because I was confident in my own ability and process to facilitate transformation.

HOW TRANSFORMATION WORKS

As a "recovering engineer," I am wild about finding ways to illustrate how things work. I love translating complicated or esoteric ideas into frameworks that people can internalize and make their own.

As I write this, I'm remembering my chemical engineering classes. There were countless diagrams in which a black box was used to represent a complex system of transformation that was taking place, chemically, within a step of a manufacturing process. For example, two chemical ingredients would go into the box, interact with each other in some way, and come out in a whole different structure.

Truth be told, although I graduated in the top 10 percent of my engineering class (I was great at math, and my skill in reading people meant I always knew what would be on the tests!) I never fully understood what I was doing. I mean, I did—but I really didn't. I couldn't comprehend *why* I should care about these chemicals going in and out, let alone why the fluid in the center of a pipe flows faster than the fluid at the edges!

In other words, I had no great interest in chemical reactions. But if we think of transformation as alchemy, it can give us a wonderful and simplified perspective on how transformation works.

The black box, in this case, isn't a mysterious reaction between two or more chemical compounds. It is the transformational container in which you work your magic—aka, the combination of your unique Sourced Energy, healing gifts, and various modalities.

I know, I know. You're thinking, "Great, Darla, but what the heck is *actually* inside that black box?"

The answer is … It doesn't matter. The box represents your work with your clients. Transformation happens inside it. The "ingredients" are just details.

The more you can think of transformation this way, the easier it will be to offer and sell it! Whether your "box" involves combustion or evaporation—or EFT tapping or pole dancing— is almost irrelevant to the bigger picture, as long as it works.

Many modalities, experiences, and approaches can work beautifully to create transformation—as long as they are applied within The Anatomy of a Transformation framework.

The first step to facilitating transformation is *owning the fact that your work transforms.* Transformation doesn't teach your client all the answers. It doesn't transfer a specific skill. It doesn't get stuff done for them. It doesn't design a website, or file taxes, or teach marketing strategies. Instead, it aligns your client with Source, and *energetically connects them with the results they want in any and all of those areas.*

THE ANATOMY OF A TRANSFORMATION

So, what actually happens inside the black box? The three stages of *The Anatomy of a Transformation*!

1. Commitment
2. The Sourced Experience
3. Integration

Imagine that within the black box, there are three smaller boxes that look like this:

THE ANATOMY OF A TRANSFORMATION

In the first stage, Commitment, your client (or retreat attendee) gets clear on what they truly want (or don't want) and declares their commitment to their own transformation.

In the second stage, The Sourced Experience, they move through a three-step, experiential process to birth a new, beautiful energy that wants to come through. This is the heart of the transformation, and moves the client from Default to Sourced Energy.

In the third stage, Integration, your client brings this new Sourced Energy into their daily life.

In the next six chapters, I'll be breaking down the Anatomy with specific examples of how it works and how to recognize it in sessions and retreats with clients. Understanding these stages will help you attract and work with fabulous clients on their journeys to self-empowerment, and help you draw the right boundaries for your work together. You'll avoid codependent client relationships, and also have the courage to challenge your clients in appropriate ways.

Here is a quick overview of the three stages of the Anatomy.

STAGE 1: COMMITMENT

As a prerequisite to transformation, you *must* have a commitment. Any attempt to bypass your client's internal commitment will create frustration for you both.

There are two aspects of Commitment: discomfort and desire.

To create a commitment to truly transform, your clients must be present to the discomfort of where they are now, present to their desire for what they truly want, or some combination of the two.

The gap between your client's discomfort with their current situation and the desire for something more will be the foundation for their commitment. Until they are present to this gap, they won't be willing to see what they need to do to transform.

However, back to our "black box" visual: we don't need to know the "how" of a transformation in order to commit to it. We don't even need to know what, specifically, is going to transform—but we *must* be committed to welcoming the transformation when it shows up. I saw this willingness in Kristy on our first call; she was ready to change, even if she didn't know exactly what changes she was committing to. That's why she became so emotional when she said yes to our work together!

If we knew beforehand what was going to happen along the road of our transformation, we might not welcome it. I've had plenty of uncomfortable transformations that I would not have willingly signed up for—yet, on the other side, I couldn't imagine the energy shift happening any other way. This is why we want our clients to commit to transformation first. The "how" will always come once commitment is established.

STAGE 2: THE SOURCED EXPERIENCE

Once your client is committed, transformation can begin. Enter The Sourced Experience.

There are two types of Sourced Experiences: the kind that "happens to you" in your life, and the *curated* Sourced Experience (such as a retreat or a coaching program) that is designed for transformation.

Both of these tend to follow the same three-part flow, which is Release, Receive, and Rise. Curated Sourced Experiences tend to be less painful as they are committed to beforehand and intentionally guided.

THE ANATOMY OF A TRANSFORMATION

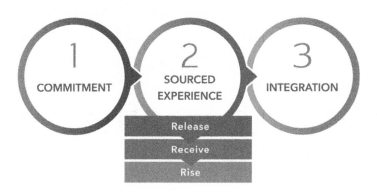

During a Sourced Experience, your client will Release control, and surrender their ideas about the "right" way to do things (or even what needs to be done). When they do this, they can Receive a new Truth about something in their Default Energy that has been previously hidden from view. As coaches, we can validate that truth, opening up a new space for Sourced Energy. From there, the client can create a commitment to Rise into a whole new energy field. Finally, they can solidify this new energy through an experience of it, which is why it's called a Sourced Experience.

Understanding this flow is critical to guiding the process, and so I've devoted a chapter in Part II to each of these parts.

STAGE 3: INTEGRATION

Once the client has an experience of embodying Sourced Energy, it's time to integrate it. They must make changes in various areas of their lives to reflect this new energy. As we saw in Brittany's story in Chapter One, just because someone has shifted, doesn't mean that the people in their lives have gotten the memo.

Most people have no experience with holding a new energy when others don't understand or don't want it. At this point, many revert back to the old ways of being. However, this is also where the magic happens, and where your client will start seeing "real world" results from their transformation.

NOT ALL TRANSFORMATION IS CREATED EQUAL

As you may already be aware, not all coaches who talk about transformation actually deliver it in their work. You may even be sick of the word "transformation," as it has become so popular among those who don't practice it. (For this reason, I often use the phrase "transmutation of energy" with my clients; this phrase feels deeper and more accurate.)

Many teach motivation and positive thinking and call it transformation (or mindset), but they don't go deep enough to help clients see the challenging truths they've been avoiding and heal at a core level.

Others teach fabulous systems or strategies that a client can model. They expect the client to execute the appropriate action steps and create results, *whether or not* they are energetically aligned with the system. This works to an extent, but it can't create a true Sourced result.

Still other providers offer deep healing work, but don't know how to make the outcome of that healing practical and actionable in clients' lives. They may inadvertently perpetuate the idea that the client needs to keep healing because the initial shifts don't "stick" in the real world. Transformation feels great, but we also need to make it practical. We are human beings who are meant to experience being human through our actions and relationships!

In my company, we "make the sublime practical." We coach our clients and retreat groups to hear what Source is offering, to fully experience the energies they have been bringing and wish to bring, and to harness their authentic power in the world. We then offer programs that support the *integration* of this new energetic power into their current lives. As you'll discover, this part is key to creating lasting transformation.

Over the course of this book, you will learn how to lead from Source in your business, so that you can help others transform. This is possible whether you work with people around their businesses, careers, relationships, sex lives, health, public speaking, creative expression, or money. It's also possible if you're teaching sales skills through improvisational theater, pole dancing for inner resilience for moms, or any other wildly-specific client niche. Clients in any and all of these areas will benefit from stepping into your black box of transformation!

Since you're reading this, I'm guessing that the type of transformation I'm describing—the deep, lasting, change-your-life-forever kind—is already part of your magic at some level. You may have already helped clients make these kinds of shifts. But you may not talk about it, and you may not think it's predictable. You may be thinking, "I never want to be one of those people who peddle transformation but don't deliver!"

As of right now, I want you to commit to bringing transformation into your work.

Remember when I said in Chapter One that you will need to transform yourself in order to hold space for your clients' transformations? It starts here. No more hiding your magic in the background. No more sneaking it in through the side door or selling them what they want to give them what they need.

It's your time to be Sourced and seen!

LIVING SOURCED

If you want to consistently Shift the Field for others, you need to live in your own Sourced Energy. When we follow what is alive for us and lean into it, we become capable of deeper trust. We trust ourselves to handle how our lives unfold. We lose our fears around making "wrong" decisions for ourselves and with our clients, because we know that "wrong" only exists to show us where we are still operating in Default Energy.

This is important to understand because it will help you step into your magic.

As a leader who lives Sourced, your intuition is a beautiful asset to all of your work. (We'll speak more about intuition in Part III). It can help you to be a revealer of truth to your clients in a loving and supportive way. Eventually, it can lead you to a level of expansion your mind could never have predicted.

Kristy discovered that she was no longer willing to offer services that caused her to travel more than she would like, and that caused her clients to make more money but be less happy. What she realized on our initial call was that her *discomfort* with her current circumstances and her *desire* for this new approach were collectively greater than her fear of change.

We didn't talk at first about what changes she would need to make, because at that point neither of us knew what those changes were! I could have given her plenty of good advice about things like pricing, program structure, etc., but none of that would have made a difference to her. It would have given her mind something to latch on to, but would not have transformed her results. After all, she'd already read my first book, *Retreat and Grow Rich*, so she understood retreat-based business models. What she needed wasn't information, but transformation.

In order to begin that process, she needed to make Commitment, both emotional and financial, that caused her to be willing to look at who she would need to become, energetically, to lead the business she dreamed of.

Once committed, Kristy had to Release her attachments to her old ways of being, Release the perception of control she'd been operating under since childhood, Release the idea that trusting another human being would be impossible, and Release the notion that she should be able to do it all herself.

In this place of Release, she could Receive a new Truth—about herself, and the judgments she'd held about herself that she didn't even know were there.

The Release happened to occur for Kristy hanging on a rope in a dark cavern in the jungles of Mexico. (As I said, I could not have predicted this, even though I knew it would happen.)

Until that point, Kristy had done such a good job putting herself together professionally that she thought she would never have to face the shame she carried within. She thought that, if she couldn't see it, it would simply go away. And *that shame* was the reason she was stuck—in her business, and on the rope.

Kristy was beautiful, well-dressed, and perfectly manicured. Her work was polished and professional. No one would have ever guessed that Kristy grew up with very little in terms of both money and attention. No one, as she tells it, ever showed her how to take care of herself. As a child, she'd kept to herself socially—so much so that she wasn't even aware that she didn't smell good.

There had been no one in Kristy's life who viewed her as special or magical.

She'd found her way to using drugs, and took the fastest path out of school possible, not even graduating. And when she eventually found a career that she was good at and began to excel, she was quick to cover up her past and pretend it didn't matter.

This worked really well when she was selling systems. She'd learned the systems through her previous career experience and knew what worked. She invested to educate herself about how to run a business and taught her clients to run an efficient ship. It was all very practical and logical.

But when she began to feel pulled to share more about leadership and mindset, and help people actually be happy in their work, she began to realize that she had to embody that too.

To understand what the company owners she was working with really wanted beyond money, she needed them to get really vulnerable with her. But how could she do that when she wasn't ready to get vulnerable with herself?

That vulnerability crashed down on her halfway up that rope. She was paralyzed with fear and couldn't even speak. Suddenly I saw it. "This is where she stops," I said to myself.

Kristy had not been honest with us about her fear—of the cave we rappelled into, or of the ladder and rope we would use to climb out. She'd been terrified, but had kept it to herself. She started out strong on her way up, but soon her body couldn't suppress her internal stress any longer. Suddenly, she couldn't move. Her way of approaching the situation—"keep it together and power through"—was no longer working, just like it was no longer working in her business.

She Released control and Received her Truth.

The reality was that she had never sat with, let alone transformed, the things that had happened in her childhood. She was a master at hiding her past.

No one had supported her, so she was not used to asking for support.

Because she'd learned quickly to hide her own fear and run from her experience of shame by pretending to having it all together, she was literally unable to communicate her fears around this physical challenge. Instead, she froze.

She was able to see the parallel to the place in her business where she'd stopped herself. The place where she had been hiding her fear, clamming up, and stopping herself from sharing her truths.

She would need to expose these vulnerable parts of herself to be able to hold space for her clients and do the work she wanted to do.

With the support of our experience, Kristy now had the opportunity to embrace a new approach—to shift her energy and become someone new.

First, she had to find her voice and let us know what she was experiencing. She was fully supported by our guides in getting up the ladder and off the rope. And with the support structure of The Anatomy of a Transformation, she was able to process the experience and step into her Sourced Energy of being *love, light, protected,* and *feeling good.*

This was such a breakthrough over the nervous, pushing, "proving" energy she had been building from before. This new Sourced Energy allowed Kristy to boldly share what she truly felt was important for her clients. She could reveal the details of her own journey because she had released her insecurity about her childhood experiences while on retreat. It felt good to be able share so much more of herself, even if it was scary at first.

She moved through the black box of transformation and came out the other side in alignment with her goals. As she started to Rise in this energy, one by one her clients transitioned from being systems clients to being leadership clients, committed to their own transformations.

This is what I am going to teach you to do with your clients, in detail, over the course of this book. We'll explore how to create the initial Commitment to transformation, how to create a space for your clients to Release control, how to expertly guide them to Receive the Truth behind what they are experiencing, and how to discern the Sourced Energy that wants to Rise through them at this time.

What will be possible for you, your work, and your mission in this world when you stop selling the business plan, the how-to checklist, or the five-step system, and start aligning clients energetically with Sourced-level results? You're about to find out!

PART II

THE ANATOMY OF A TRANSFORMATION

CHAPTER THREE
COMMITMENT

*B*etsy was a Human Resources professional who'd had enough of the corporate life. She loved the concept of being a support person for people's careers and helping them to love their work while working harmoniously with their teams—but ten years into her career, she became clear that the work she was doing did *not* light her up. In fact, it drained her.

As she shared with me on our initial call, many of the policies and protocols she was forced to follow required her to take actions that she didn't believe were right for the humans involved. She wanted to create a new company—a company where she could help employers hold their relationships with their employees in a different light.

I vibed with everything she was saying. I couldn't wait to help her break through her fear of striking out on her own and design the business of her dreams!

However, after a frustrating six weeks of working together, I discovered something that was devastating to me at the time. Betsy wasn't breaking through. In fact, she didn't *want* to break through.

In her mind, there was nothing that needed to change *within her* to get this new result. In her perception, the problem was all *out there*. She wanted things to be different, but she didn't actually want to *do things differently*.

Her vibration was aligned with results that frustrated her. But instead of Shifting the Field and opening to new possibilities, she wanted to use the same old approach she was using in her job to create her new business. She was imagining that this was all it would take for her to be less frustrated and more fulfilled.

I knew in every cell of my being that this was the wrong approach. And so, at my suggestion (and by mutual concession) Betsy and I parted ways.

I never found out what happened to Betsy and her new business idea.

So ... what went wrong? Was the problem with Betsy, and her lack of willingness to make change? Or was the problem actually with me?

Everything is Sourced; therefore, there was nothing wrong at all. Betsy was on her perfect journey, and she got what she got from our energy exchange. And I—well, I got a great lesson and a story I've told to my retreat leader clients for years. (By the way, Betsy is not her real name.)

Things spooled out with Betsy the way they did because I didn't yet fully understand The Anatomy of a Transformation, or how to create transformation predictably.

The fact was, I'd skipped over a key step in the process. I was so excited to have a new client, and I loved the idea of the business *I thought* Betsy was describing so much, that I allowed my enthusiasm to bypass the most critical step in our work together: Betsy's *commitment* to her own transformation.

This key step should happen before your client says "Yes!" to your work together. If it doesn't, you should say "No" to the client.

THE ANATOMY OF A TRANSFORMATION

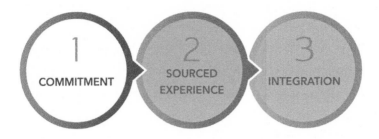

Without Commitment, there can be no transformation.

Commitment can show up in many ways, and does not always look the same. One person may appear nonchalant, but they are deeply committed to Shifting the Field, while another may seem to be diligently committed by doing a lot of things, only to reveal through their actions that they are not actually committed to their transformation at all.

Our job as transformational leaders is to help clients generate their own commitment to the outcome they are seeking—one that is strong enough that they will be willing to see the truth that has up until now been hidden from them, and which they will have to see and acknowledge in order to Release, Receive, and Rise.

Unless and until you become a master at facilitating client commitment, your transformational business will struggle. There are many talented healers and coaches who, given a committed client, can work wonders. The problem is that most potential clients aren't yet committed to their own transformations. If they were, *they would already be changing their lives!*

In her book *Wealth Through Workshops*, Callan Rush notes that just 3 percent of the people who would benefit from your services are actively seeking a solution like yours. Three percent!

I want you to get present to the discomfort of that. If you're struggling to bring in clients, you aren't understanding your job as a transformational leader.

You may be operating under the assumption that your job is to facilitate transformation (and therefore a particular outcome) for people who want it. You may be nodding your head, thinking, "Yes, people will transform with me, and get new outcomes. That is what I do."

But I'd like to suggest that your job is to create a desire for, and a commitment to, transformation in people who are seeking a new outcome.

But if only 3 percent of those who need your services are actually *aware* that they need to transform and are actively seeking someone like you to help them do it—in other words, are *committed* to their own transformation—what about everyone else?

Offering a service for people who are already committed means that you are only serving 3 percent of your potential market. Instead, think less about serving those 3 percent (they'll find you, even if you're hiding under a rock!) and instead consider what it would take to help all of your other potential clients become committed.

Callan estimates that about 30 percent of people who need your services will never want to transform. So, how can you help that remaining 67 percent commit to transformation?

You tap into two things: their discomfort, and their desire.

DISCOMFORT AND DESIRE

There are two key things that lead to Commitment: discomfort and desire. Let's start with discomfort.

Discomfort—aka, mental or physical uneasiness—is a major reason we commit to transformation. When we are *present to* our discomfort, and it is greater than our fear of what it will take to transform, we will commit to doing whatever it takes, or *being* whoever it takes, to make that change.

However, we humans are masters at avoiding our discomfort. In our modern world we use busy-ness, obligation, and various tools for numbing ourselves to avoid being present to the things that make us squirm.

Before you read any further, pause to ask yourself how you are feeling right now. It is likely you are not in major discomfort, since you're likely seated somewhere, relaxing and reading this book.

Still, pause. Breathe.

Okay, great.

Now, I'm going to share a short list of five areas where people commonly experience discomfort. As you read the list, pause after each area and get present to how you feel in that area. Notice any sensations in your body. Notice your thoughts.

I'll meet you on the other side.

Five common areas of discomfort

1) *Food and movement.* Am I feeding my body things it loves and thrives on and moving it regularly to keep myself connected to good feelings in my beautiful body?
2) *Money, money, money.* Do I feel good about the money I am receiving and where and how I am directing it, with a healthy relationship to the abundance all around me?
3) *Love.* Do I feel good about the people in my life? Do I see them and feel seen by them, and experience the types of energy exchanges I truly desire, keeping my love real and current?

4) *Life purpose.* Do I know why I get up in the morning and feel confident that the way I expend my vital life force energy each day is in alignment with my dearest values?

5) *Self-expression.* Do I know that I am showing up fully as myself, in my appearance and my action? Do I feel the joy of being in my own skin and allowing my body and my words to move as I desire?

How did that go?

Did examining one or more of these areas make you feel some slight discomfort because you know you are not fully aligned with what you want in that area? Did you suddenly remember that you're *very* uncomfortable in one or more areas, but you've gotten so good at ignoring it that it's been completely off your radar all day?

Congratulations. You are normal.

The goal of this exercise is to demonstrate how becoming present to our discomfort, even just for a moment, amplifies our discomfort! It is always there, but most days we just slide past it.

This is true for your potential clients as well. Unless they are in that 3 percent of already-committed seekers we talked about, there is a good chance that they really do want a different outcome, but haven't stopped to get present to it yet!

When I was first starting out, I was so focused on growing the business that I ignored my health. Initially, this wasn't a conscious choice, I just neglected myself. Then I started gaining weight, and my pants all got tight. I put on yoga pants and kept working.

I had become aware of my discomfort (tight pants), and then consciously made a choice to ignore the discomfort by changing the clothes I wore. At that time, I couldn't imagine trying to make time to do better grocery shopping or to go to the gym, so I employed a strategy (thank you yoga pants!) that allowed me to avoid the discomfort for just a bit longer.

Admit it. At some point, in some area of your life, you've done this, too.

It's okay. We can't address all of our issues at once, and there are times that it is completely appropriate to avoid our discomfort in one area to keep moving forward in another. The goal is not perfection, but progress. Yet I also believe our lives expand and grow in direct proportion to the courage we exhibit in being present to our discomfort.

And here is the great news: when we make a shift in one area of life, every other area will shift along with it. When we shift our energy, it permeates everything. So, if you read the list above and felt a little uncomfortable in quite a few areas, have no fear. Choose one to transform, and the others will follow.

As a leader, it's important that you get good at being present to discomfort in your own life and using it as leverage to transform. Otherwise, you'll struggle to help your clients do it. You have to "walk the talk," as they say. And, once your potential client's discomfort becomes greater than their fear of change, they will become committed to the transformation you are offering ... not just the results.

Your clients can also be pulled toward commitment by desire.

Desire—aka, a conscious impulse toward something that promises enjoyment or satisfaction—is a powerful motivator. Its root is Latin, with *de* (meaning *of*) and *sider/sidus* (meaning *heavenly body*).

In other words, desire is *of the heavenly body,* or *of Spirit,* and can be trusted as a whisper from your soul. It's a call toward growth, transformation, and expansion.

Most people don't know this interpretation. Instead, we are systematically taught that desire is evil, sinful, or unethical, and that people who follow their desires are bad, wrong, selfish, or just not team players.

I want to be clear: doing or taking whatever we want, even if it hurts others, is not true desire. Sourced desires will never violate the rights of others. A true desire (of Spirit) will never lead you astray. In fact, as a leader, understanding your own desire is an important aspect of living Sourced.

However, your desire may make others uncomfortable. When you follow your desire, you will open up a new Sourced Energy. Moving through life in this energy will cause others to get present to the gap between where they are and where they want to be, and their own discomfort around that gap. Because they are, like all of us, masterful at avoiding discomfort, many will want to make your desire wrong so that they don't have to change. Thus, the human habit of shaming people for following their desires.

I could go on for pages about the myriad ways religions and governments have used this shame around desire (internal connection to Source) to control people and populations. I'll save that for another book—but for now, understand that this habit of shaming desire is deeply ingrained within us. In fact, we tend to avoid being present to our desire almost as strongly as we avoid our discomfort!

For example …

You may desire to put nourishing foods in your body, but being called "high maintenance" when ordering at a restaurant brings on feelings of shame. So, you just eat what everyone else is eating.

You may desire to make an abundance of money so you never have to limit your decisions because of cash flow, but you've been told all your life that wealthy people are selfish and being selfish would make you ashamed. So, you avoid bringing in the money, or give it all away before it's even landed in your bank account.

You may desire close, intimate relationships in your life, but you're afraid that if you start expressing more authentically, people will find you strange or inappropriate.

You may want to change your career or business to be in alignment with your true purpose, but you don't want to make your spouse uncomfortable about the level of risk involved.

You may want to dress or walk or act differently, but watching the comment streams on others' Instagram posts makes you terrified of putting yourself out there.

However, none of these are reasons to ignore your desire!

When our desire becomes greater than our fear of change, we commit to our transformation.

For some people, it's the discomfort that moves them. They are no longer willing to allow another year, month, or week, to go by with the same results. Something causes them to recognize, and get present to, their discomfort, and they say, "I want out of this!"

Others are propelled by desire. They see or recognize something they want, often reflected in another person, and something clicks. They say, "I *want* that. I am *called* to that. I can no longer remain here when I am meant to be over there."

For most, some combination of discomfort and desire creates the commitment.

THE GAP

The "gap" is a common term in the world of transformation. It represents the difference between where you are and where you want to be.

This is such an incredibly simple concept that people often overlook it. We think that to start a business and bring in new clients we need to teach all sorts of new and novel concepts, be the first to articulate something, or make our methods sound brainy and intellectual. But the truth is, if we can master this simple idea of "the gap," we won't need to sell our concepts and processes. Those are just tools that we will employ to help our clients close the gap.

The gap is visible when your client becomes present to the discomfort of where they are and holds it in contrast to their desired future.

You may notice I continue to use the word *present*. This is important.

As I explored Merriam-Webster's definitions for the word *present*, I found that the one most suited to what I mean is marked as obsolete! That definition is *attentive*. The closest non-obsolete definition I found to my intent was *being in view or at hand*.

Being present (and specifically being present to the gap) is allowing ourselves to *be with*, and *be attentive to*, that which we are really thinking and feeling at any moment. We are not trying to avoid or dodge what is true for us or for our clients— the circumstances, results, thoughts, or feelings. We are able to simply *be with* them.

I don't want you (or your clients) to *think about* the gap, or intellectualize the gap, or brainstorm ideas to close the gap. We can do this all day long. Our minds are bright and capable, and can come up with many plans for closing the gap *without actually being present to it*.

In fact, intellectualizing the gap is an exercise in avoiding discomfort. We're trying to find the answer without actually exploring the pain.

What? You're not organized? Here are five tools you can use to know where to put everything and find it when you need it.

Need to lose weight? Eat less calories and exercise.

Want to make more money? Try my ten-step social media marketing system!

How many of your clients have found themselves jumping on the next trendy bandwagon to no avail? And how many times have they found themselves right back in the same discomfort, and in an even worse circumstance than when they started?

The intense need to avoid discomfort is behind every major issue we have, personally and systemically, in our society. For example, we haven't solved our issues with systemic racism in America because white America is collectively *unwilling to be present to their discomfort* around race issues. Affirmative action and other measures are intellectualizations (helpful, for sure, but not transformational). They're strategies to combat a problem that no one has been willing to actually feel into. This is the definition of privilege. In order to transform, we must allow ourselves to experience the deep discomfort of racism's impact on all of us. More, we have to go deep enough to make this discomfort bigger than our fear of releasing our privilege and transforming into a more equal, equitable society. Only then can we Shift the Field.

(Note that I use "we" to include myself and my own privilege, not to exclude the BIPOC leaders reading this book. You have been present to this discomfort for far too long, without nearly enough support. I see you, and I commit to staying present to my discomfort and work the principles in this book, actively and out loud, to transform racism. I say this with full presence to my own discomfort at the risk of actually putting these words to the page without knowing the how. That is how transformation works.)

As you can see from the above examples, you can address your problems, and your clients' problems, at the level of the rational mind, but that will rarely create the kinds of change you're looking for. Presence with discomfort and desire is the only way to go deeper, shift the energy, and begin the process of real transformation.

The commitment to going deeper serves us and our clients at an individual level and can serve at a collective level by transforming businesses and even global problems when we get the right people on board with the commitment.

Our job, when we begin the process of Shifting the Field, is not to help our clients analyze the past and what got them here; this will likely lead to justification and affirming limitations. Nor is it to try to solve the problem of how to create a different future (creating a new future comes later). Our job is simply to be in the present moment: to bring forward the energy of what is—both discomfort and desire—and sit with that energy.

As we've explored, being present to discomfort is different than rationalizing or intellectualizing it. In the same way, being present to a desire is different than daydreaming about the desire.

This is subtle but important. We daydream all day long. We imagine what-if scenarios in our mind. We think about what would be different if only some circumstance (which we likely think is outside of our control) would change.

Being present to a desire means taking it out of the future and bringing it into the present. It's helping your client experience what it feels like *in their energy field* to have their desire be real and alive right now.

Believe it or not, most people don't realize that they are thinking about a desire as a conditional future that they will somehow create if and when life lines up for them. This thinking actually *ensures* that they will not have the desire now, because they are energetically keeping it in the future!

When we help our clients to get present to their desire, we hold space for them to bring that desire into their energy field and experience what it would be like to fulfill that desire, right now, in their body, in the present moment. Everything they create in the future actually gets created first in their body in the present moment.

Most people won't be able to hold this without support (if they could, they would have done so already). Something is in the way of them having that desire. Releasing whatever is in the way is the work you will do inside your "black box" during Stage 2 of their transformation. But in order for your unique alchemical shift to occur inside that black box, your client needs to be present to the gap—to the difference between their current situation and desired outcome—and commit to doing whatever it takes to bridge it.

Their discomfort may be enough.

Their desire may be enough.

But the combination of the two will almost always create commitment.

If there is no discomfort, and no desire, then there is likely no commitment. And guess what? That's no problem! People are welcome to stay right where they are, for as long as they want.

For example, two years into my business, I still had no commitment to losing weight. My pants were really tight, but that discomfort wasn't enough to motivate me to transform. I just kept buying bigger, stretchier outfits and went on with my life … until a new, seemingly unrelated desire showed up in my world.

I had started to study intuition and was allowing my own intuition to play a bigger role in guiding my business and client work. I was surprised by the way my intuition was speaking, but it wasn't totally reliable. Sometimes I could hear my intuition clearly, and sometimes I couldn't.

I began to wonder: would putting better food into my body increase my intuition?

You see, looking perfect in a dress, while nice, wasn't a true motivator for me. And, as a thirty-something with zero health issues, healing and longevity weren't either. But being better for my clients, becoming the best leader I could be, and leaning into this cool new thing called "intuition?" These things mattered to me.

Once I connected my new desire to my health, I was committed. I became one of the 3 percent, and I sought out a health coach to support me to make changes.

Looking back, I wonder: if someone had presented me with a marketing message that linked physical health and increased intuition, with an outcome of being a better coach and leader, would I have listened? I like to think that I would have. And, if that message had existed at that time, I likely would have connected the dots and found my commitment sooner—and I probably would have hired the coach who had helped me to see it.

LACK OF COMMITMENT = DEFAULT ENERGY

As we've learned, when people aren't committed to their transformation, it's almost always because they have not yet allowed themselves to get present to the gap between their current discomfort and future desire.

But *why* is this happening?

Part of it is that we are all balancing various commitments and priorities. Just like me with my weight gain, not all things we desire have hit our radar as "musts"—either because we are busy in other areas, or because we haven't connected them to a desire big enough to motivate us to change.

But there's more to it than that.

Once your client gets committed, they open themselves up to Stage 2 of The Anatomy of a Transformation. This is where they will surrender control and Release their old ways of being in order to Receive and Rise.

True commitment to transformation means being willing to "go there," and see truths that we have previously been unwilling or unable to see. Your subconscious mind and ego know this and will fight to keep to your old commitments—your Default Energy—in place.

Remember, ego is trying to keep us safe. Moving out of our comfort zones does not feel safe. When we commit to transformation, we are committing to a wild ride. We know the destination we desire, but our conscious minds have no idea where the path will take us, or what challenges we will face. This is good, because if we did, we probably wouldn't go! But our ego knows that things are about to get shaken up—and so, it does its best to keep us distracted, because it is powerless in the face of full presence.

This is why presence is a necessary ingredient for Shifting the Field. It is the only way to get the ego to relent long enough for change to take hold.

More, whatever energy shift is about to take place, it likely won't be convenient. Maybe it will challenge us. Maybe it will challenge those around us. And maybe it won't be challenging at all, but will blow our old identity out of the water and require, at the very least, a new wardrobe.

And so, we find our own ways to avoid transformation: staying busy, ruminating on the past, daydreaming about a future we aren't taking steps to create. And yet, all the magic we want happens when we get present.

When you—as a coach, mentor, leader, and especially salesperson—can bring someone to presence with what is there for them, you are giving them the biggest, most amazing gift ever.

Which may be quite uncomfortable.

ASSUMPTIONS AND PROJECTIONS

Remember my client Betsy? Our work didn't create transformation for her because, when it really came down to the wire, she was not committed.

She seemed committed. She had discomfort (*I don't like the way my company is treating the humans in their organization but I don't have the power to change it because of the rules of HR*), and she had desire (*I want to be able to work with people the way I want to work with them*). But she didn't have *real* commitment.

Looking back, I can see that, in our work together, I didn't get her present to the real gap that was happening in her world. Instead, I made assumptions and projections, and transposed my own experience onto hers. This created the appearance of presence, but not real presence.

You see, I could relate to Betsy's feelings about not aligning with the values of her company. This was one reason I'd left the corporate world, and a primary reason many of my clients chose to make change in their lives. Because of my prior experience, I assumed that I knew what this misalignment meant to Betsy, too.

I asked her a bit about what she didn't like about her job. But then, I inserted my own opinions about the rest, rather than asking what it meant to her, on the inside. I didn't take time to understand her personal worldview and specifically what wasn't working for her. Rather I projected my own opinions and worldview and assumed that what worked for me would also work for her.

Betsy said that her desire was to run her business her way, outside the rules of her company. Again, because I understood that desire from my own experience and perspective, I skipped over getting to the heart of her desire and understanding why it was important *to her*.

It was obvious from the start that getting Betsy the results she desired was going to necessitate a massive shift in energy. Her vibe was very heavy, and her language and vibration revealed that she had a victim perspective about what was happening. She felt that the industry was wrong, that her company was wrong, and that she was at the mercy of both. She thought the answer would be to leave the circumstances—but, as you know, we bring our energy with us into new circumstances.

Without becoming present to the fact that her Default Energy had actually created her first set of circumstances, Betsy didn't realize that starting a new business without shifting her energy would eventually re-create the same experience. She would have attracted clients that made her feel powerless—or no clients at all.

I noticed this low energy when we first spoke, but in our initial conversation I skipped over explicitly talking about it. In my excitement about helping her transform, and in my assumptions and projections about her experiences, I forgot to confirm that she was truly committed to closing this gap.

In the end, Betsy wasn't willing to see that she was actually the source of her own experience, take responsibility for her current circumstances, and free herself to create something new.

With a few short questions in our first call, I could have discovered that she really didn't see a need to shift. Her desire was to create a company from the same energy that she was experiencing in her job. She would continue to be frustrated by the "rules" that society was putting on her, and not actually have a happy outcome. And that was entirely her right, and her choice.

But I also have a choice. And I don't want to help someone build a business that will make them unhappy. I choose to work with clients who are committed to closing the *real* gap.

If I don't stay present to my own desire—to work with committed clients—I end up inadvertently participating in the "sell them what they want and give them what they need" model. I thought I knew what Betsy needed, but I never confirmed it with her. Instead, I decided I knew what was best. If she could shift her victim energy, I thought, she could create a business that aligned with the values she felt were being violated in her current job. But in the end, that was *my* desire, not hers.

I didn't ask her to get present to the discomfort of living a life in which her values were being consistently violated. I didn't ask her to describe what she wanted to experience and how she wanted to feel when running her business. And I didn't ask her why *she* thought she had created this current situation for herself, thus checking her level of personal responsibility.

Had I done these things, I likely would have discovered that she didn't actually believe in energy, or the idea that she had the power to change her experience of the world. She wasn't interested in the destination I was committed to for her.

THE LAW OF SACRIFICE

The Law of Sacrifice states that we must sacrifice, or give up, something of a lower nature in order to receive something of a higher nature.

When we dream about our goals, we don't always think about what we will need to give up to create them. In Betsy's case, reaching her goals would necessitate giving up her habit of being a victim to her circumstances, her employer, and society. While it seems like that would be an easy choice, she was clearly getting something out of staying in that energy. Her victim story had been working for her in some way for a long time, or else she would have already released it.

For me, holding on to extra weight when I was growing my business worked for me as well. That extra weight made me feel safer. As an overweight kid, I'd learned that people didn't notice me as much as they did thinner people. My weight was a buffer against the world. So, as I was becoming more visible—and more vulnerable—in my business, the extra weight helped balance my fearful feelings by allowing me to feel hidden and comfortable. To achieve the goal of being more tuned in to my body, I had to give up that perception of safety that the weight provided.

There are many examples I could share to demonstrate this, and I am sure you have many of your own, as you've navigated your own transformation. Sacrifice may come tangibly in the form of relationships, living situations, jobs, or even careers that were established in old, Default Energy. Sacrifice is revealed in giving up things like control, safety, our perceived identity, our sense of responsibility, etc.

The main thing to note is that if someone is not immediately saying 'yes' to go on a transformational journey, it doesn't mean they don't want *and* need it. It simply may mean that, deep down, they know that saying yes to their transformation means saying yes to the sacrifice, too. Even if they—and you—don't know what it is, you can rest assured that something that used to make them feel safe will need to be released.

So, even though the transformation you're offering may feel exciting and freeing, hold your clients in compassion as they make the decision to move forward. Help them stay present to the gap as they commit to an unknown sacrifice and say yes to shifting into their Sourced Energy field.

COMMITMENT IS NON-LINEAR

Our client, Bonnie, committed to a year-long coaching program which kicked off with a virtual retreat. She'd booked an Airbnb to give herself lots of space to be present with us and dive into the material without distraction. On the way to her space, it seemed everything was trying to stop her: weather, traffic, you name it. She became so angry at the obstacles that continuously dropped in her path that she considered turning around and going home. Thankfully, she texted me to let me know she thought she would be giving up and not attending. I was able to help her stay the course, and to trust that all was unfolding perfectly inside her commitment.

When you have a "transformation first" program, your clients' commitments to different aspects of the program create the boundaries of the container you hold for them. Each retreat, or training, or session with you gives a space and a time for Spirit to show up and work with your client in their personal divine curriculum. In Bonnie's case, the roadblocks on her journey created so much anger within her; this was interesting information, because she would have told you she was not an "angry" person.

Her experience was the perfect setup for her discovery at the retreat. She was able to see how her anger was actually directed at her father, who had thrown up roadblocks to her self-expression and voice when she was a child. She had a big commitment to receiving lots of money, and one layer of the transformation she needed was to reclaim her voice so she could feel worthy of being compensated for her gifts.

When we are on the verge of Shifting the Field, there is *so* much energy coming to the surface to be looked at and transformed. Our natural instinct will almost always be to back away. Often, at the beginning of a program, I'll hear all kinds of excuses from clients: "I can't make it," "Something came up," etc.

This is why we ask people to commit. As a facilitator, be prepared to hold the space even when your client, or their circumstance, makes transforming seem like a terrible idea!

Some people in your programs might be completely opposite. They will commit and go all in, Shifting the Field rather quickly at the beginning of your work together. They may immediately begin to see major results. The flow opens up. They Rise, as intended.

And then, things may begin to feel uncomfortable. Their ego or Default Energy may pop up and say, "It can't be this easy. You don't deserve this!" Then, they get distracted from continuing to integrate their Sourced Energy.

Sometimes this distraction might manifest as some sort of idea or project that will keep them busy but not necessarily move them forward. Alternatively, someone in their life may create a distraction that suddenly feels more important than their own commitment. They may also simply think that the initial transformation they experienced was enough, and take their foot off the transformational gas.

I've seen this a lot. A client has big results right away, then they simply … stop. Then, as their program approaches an end, they freak out a bit, realizing that they must transform *now*. They need a renewed commitment to reach their full transformation.

Robin was one of these clients. When she committed to our year-long program to train and certify Sourced Retreat Masters, she was clear that she was committed to taking center stage in her life. She experienced a breakthrough quickly, and began to trust her choices rather than deferring to others who might know better.

This led her to global adventures. Her energy was vibrant and alive. She became visible as a leader in ways that felt deeply fulfilling, even if they went against the grain of her religious upbringing.

However, within the container of her program, Robin grappled with her commitment at various times. She said yes to things, only to realize that her true answer was no, and vice versa. All of this happened in a container for learning, which allowed her to play with her decisions and cement her self-trust. But still, something was off, because she wasn't earning the money she desired.

She'd come so far, and could see the next frontier, but her training with us was coming to an end. She also had quite a few assignments to turn in if she wanted to be certified. She almost stopped at this point, thinking she'd gotten all she would get from the program. But then, she renewed her commitment to her original vision and chose to finish her assignments.

In grading her assignments, we noticed a specific pattern for how Robin was showing up. She was *talking* to people *about* transformation, rather than *asking* them to get present to their own experience. Of course she didn't have committed clients paying her. There was no room for the clients in her energy field!

It turned out that while claiming her voice and getting visible was a fantastic breakthrough for her, she needed to shift how she was expressing this. Her Default Energy pattern was, "Never ask, only tell!"

Growing up, Robin learned that if she was going to get any attention she had to take it, because otherwise no one would see or acknowledge her. She also felt responsible for helping her parents solve their problems because they weren't doing so on their own. Thus, when she was "putting herself out there," she would either talk about herself (grab the attention) or tell others how to solve their problems.

She wasn't even aware that she was doing this. When something is our default, it's simply the water we swim in. But, as we've learned in this chapter, talking about ourselves and solving others' problems doesn't work to create real commitment and transformation.

In the following week I was able to provide Robin with some very specific feedback on what I was seeing. I gave her an assignment to help her get present to the impact of this Default Energy pattern. She was not able to "tell" anyone anything for forty-eight hours. Instead, she could only ask and listen.

This assignment was extremely challenging for her. It served as her Sourced Experience and brought to the surface the energy that she needed to transform—but moving through it was only possible because of her commitment to solve her mysterious sales problem and break her income barriers.

Now, Robin could share and teach, but was also free to hold space and listen. She booked more client sessions just after this breakthrough than she'd had in the entire previous year.

It's nice to think about Commitment as a one-and-done experience. We talk to a client, we help them discover their commitment, and then we sail smoothly out into our transformational sunset.

My engineering mind loves this idea. But transformation doesn't often work that way.

Gaining a clear commitment is a necessary part of your initial sales conversation with a new client. If you use automated marketing, your sales copy and funnels should be designed to help potential clients identify the gap and create commitment. (We'll talk more about how to implement the tools of The Anatomy of a Transformation in Part III of this book.)

However, once you gain that initial commitment, you will still be playing with different levels of commitment throughout your work with your client. This is why having your client commit to a container of support (i.e., a coaching program or retreat, not just one session), is so important. This container allows them the space for their ego's patterns to show up to challenge the new commitment, and for them to receive support in recommitting and moving past the places where they would have stopped in the past.

Support for the transformational journey is vital because it's so easy to lose steam around our commitments. Think of all the New Year's Resolutions that you didn't keep. Or that time you bought a book or course inspired by your newfound commitment to making a change in your life—and never finished it. This isn't because you didn't have enough willpower, or even the right tools. As we get close to the place where we need to face a truth about ourselves, it's natural to shy away, because "going there" means sacrifice and a degree of uncertainty, and our ego does not want this!

While some of your clients will move through Stage 2 of The Anatomy of a Transformation with grace while Shifting the Field and owning their Sourced Energy with ease, others will embark on a roller-coaster ride of commitment, retreat, and recommitment. Retreat can happen any time that they are getting closer to a truth they are hoping not to see. This often happens at the beginning of a program, and at the end.

Your real job as a facilitator of transformation is to be a firm container for your clients when their commitment would otherwise waver. This, more than any tool in your little black box, will create life-changing results. Do not feel like a failure if your client shows signs of lack of commitment, and don't make them wrong when they backtrack. Hold a loving and firm space and take them back to re-establish commitment.

MY FAVORITE RECOMMITMENT TOOL

Since it's so common for clients (indeed, for all of us) to waver in Commitment, I want to share with you my favorite tool for helping clients get present again to the gap between their discomfort and desire—the Commitment T-Chart (otherwise known as the Cost-Benefit T-Chart).

I actually used this tool with Bonnie when she considered skipping our first retreat. (Since she was driving at the time, I did the writing—but the rest of the process was the same). I also use it often for myself when I'm tempted to wriggle out of the gap and back into my comfort zone.

First, give your client (or yourself) full permission to *not* be committed. You can do this by saying something like, "Whether or not you attend this retreat is completely your choice. Can I help you explore the options?" Remember, no one likes to be forced into anything, and we can't drag people into transformation!

Ask your client to take out a piece of paper and draw a line down the middle. Label the left column "Cost," and the right column "Benefit."

Then, remind her of the gap she wanted to close when she joined your program, and ask her to imagine that the result she's craving is just on the other side of the present obstacle.

Now, populate the columns of the T-Chart by asking questions about both the benefits and the costs to transforming and closing that gap. For example, I said to Bonnie, "Play with me for a minute here. If you opt not to attend our retreat and get the result, what would be the cost of that decision?" Allow your client to fill up the "Cost" column with at least six to ten items. This is the price they will pay—according to the Law of Sacrifice—for *not* allowing the transformation.

Next, move to the second column. What would be the *benefit* of staying in Default Energy and not moving forward? Allow your client to answer. Usually, there are far more costs than benefits revealed in this exercise—but eventually, you will likely hit upon a benefit that is the sneaky, secret reason why your client is resisting this transformation. It's often something like, "I get to stay safe. I get to stay in control. I can avoid responsibility. I will look good (or at least not look bad)."

Once the client sees the real reason for their resistance to commitment, they get to choose. They can experience all the costs (like relationships, love, intimacy, money, freedom, self-expression, joy, etc.) in exchange for the benefit of staying safe and playing small … or they can transform.

Ninety-nine percent of the time, they will choose the transformation.

This exercise is especially powerful to do while coaching one person in a group setting. Everyone gets to witness, through this demonstration, that they are at choice in the matter of their own transformation!

In Bonnie's case, we were looking specifically at the costs and benefits of attending the retreat. But this also works beautifully when someone has identified the Default Energy they wish to shift (as we'll learn to do in Stage 2) yet are afraid to let it go. You can use this exercise to see and validate this energy pattern and list its costs and benefits in the short and long term. The person can then decide if the pattern is still working for them, or if they are ready to let it go.

DON'T GO INTO THE GAP ALONE!

The more you work with the principles in this book, the easier it will be to see where you are in your own life, stay present to your gaps, and cultivate your own commitments.

As sovereign beings, we want to be able to do this work on a continual basis—but like most things that matter, this is easier said than done.

Why? Because most people do not want to go into the gap alone.

We resist getting present to our discomfort because we must give something up to get something out of it. We resist getting present to our desire because we have learned that people will shame us for being selfish. Yet, these uncomfortable spaces are where our commitments are born.

If you're experiencing any resistance or constraint in your own life, get support for going into the gap. The more you experience this for yourself, the easier it will be to facilitate it for others. Any of the programs on my website, working with me, or with one of my team members, are a great place to start, as are programs with our certified Sourced Leaders Transformational Coaches and Retreat Masters (see the Resources section in the back of this book for more information).

Like you, your clients don't want to go into the gap alone. And while some of their problems may be solvable at a practical, logical level, you know in your soul that they need more than just practical solutions. They need energetic transformation that will shift them into alignment with the Truth of their own souls—but before they can commit to that journey, they need to know that there is someone who will, calmly and with certainty, walk with them into the gap, and stay with them in their discomfort until they find a commitment big enough to outweigh the sacrifice.

If you are the one who walks them there, without judgment and without looking away (even if you do so on a sales page or in a webinar), they will very likely hire you as the person to take them through the full journey.

And once you have that commitment, it's time for them to step into your container and Shift the Field!

CHAPTER FOUR
THE SOURCED EXPERIENCE

"Y ou know, I'm a carpenter. I can help you with that."
I still remember exactly where I was standing when I
heard those words.

It was 2003. I was clad in green army pants, a paint splat-
tered T-shirt, and God knows what else. Plaster dust? Sawdust?
Asbestos? I was sweaty, tired, and frustrated. And John knew
exactly what to say.

I didn't comprehend this at the time, and I'm sure he didn't
either, but we were about to enter into a profound and life-
changing Sourced Experience together.

John was my contractor. I was fighting with my high-
powered DeWalt drill with the circle-saw-thingy attached to
it, attempting to drill a hole in a very hard solid wood door
which separated the bedroom in Apartment 1 from the stairs to
Apartment 2 in the property I'd purchased six months earlier. I

needed to install a deadbolt, which I'd done in the past, but this door was getting the best of me.

This guy who was sent out to lay my tile (yes, I know how that sounds) would before long become my partner, then my husband, then my ex-husband in rapid succession. And in that moment when he offered to help, time stood still.

I would relive that instant many times.

Have you ever had an experience when you sense the significance of the moment even as it's happening? When you know that there is some greater information available, in the space between the reality of what's happening and this larger *something*, that you can either receive or skip over—but either way it's shaping your future?

This was one of those moments.

Two months later, John and I had another such moment.

He said, "You know, you don't have to be so strong all the time."

We were sitting on the floor in the first-level entry of the house. He was now helping me work on the place almost daily, in exchange for nothing more than beer and pizza. I was frustrated because the house, which I'd bought as a foreclosure, was requiring a lot more work than I had first thought. My natural tendency to envision what's possible, plus the large quantities of HGTV I'd been watching, made it seem like this would be an easy rehab. Plus, after interviewing a few general contractors, I decided that I could finish more quickly (and save a bunch of money) if I just filled that role myself.

Well, that was wishful thinking! Chalk one up for the professionals.

Back to that foyer floor in Apartment 1. Exhausted after patching up what was left of the wall we'd just torn down to create more flow between the entry and living areas, John and I got personal. He challenged me to consider that how I was showing up in life was not the *only* possibility.

"You don't have to be *so strong* all the time."

He was absolutely right. I *didn't* have to be so strong all the time.

He knew exactly what to say to hook me.

At that moment in my life, I needed to work on my vulnerability. (I'm still working on it, after than ten years as an entrepreneur!) But his words were an invitation to set aside the strong part of me that had been developing so beautifully in the process of this home project, alongside my other grand plans for life. What if I could let him be strong, so I didn't have to?

The thought was alluring.

John helped me finish the house—into which he moved, rent-free. After a year, we got engaged, and started planning the wedding. All was going well. I enjoyed having a partner, and at thirty-two, I was ready to settle down. John had a five-year-old son from a previous relationship, so I had an instant family. And while there were lots of red flags from his past—including his ex-wife, who showed up screaming on our doorstep in the middle of the night, for reasons I still don't understand—we were finding our groove together.

However, in the weeks leading up to the wedding, his behavior changed. He was kind of creepy with my sister when she visited. He didn't come home one night after leaving to pick up a movie, leaving me and his son at home frantically calling hospitals and police stations in search of him. I even tried to call off the wedding for a week, but when I spoke with him, he refused to cancel or even delay it—and somehow, I let him talk me into going through with it. It was like, "Okay, well, if you don't agree with me, I guess I have to *marry* you."

Uh, hello?

But that was how it went down. The invitations were out, and our guests' travel plans were made. If I called off the wedding, everyone would know I had made a huge mistake. What would they think? On the other hand, what would those friends who knew the things he'd been doing think if I *did* go through with it?

And then, there was John's son. Oh, how I loved him. If I cancelled the wedding, it would crush him. I remember thinking to myself, in yet another of those time-stands-still moments I spoke about earlier, "It's okay if the rest of *my* life isn't that great. *His* life will be better because of me."

The woman I am today can hardly believe that I was willing to think in this way. Most of my friends and clients wouldn't recognize me in this story. But at that time, not only was I willing to think this way—it was *natural* for me to consider everyone else's needs before my own.

And so, two years after the moment I let him drill my door, John and I were married. Six months after that, we separated; in another six months, we were divorced. I was left with a broken heart, a towering stack of bills, and a whole new perspective on life.

SOURCED EXPERIENCES GIVE YOU WHAT YOU NEED TO GROW

At the time I met John I was feeling really good. I had taken a bunch of programs at Landmark Education and was on a leadership track there. I had discovered the world of possibility and knew that I could create anything I wanted in my life. For the first time, I could see a path to living on purpose and truly being seen.

And while all of this was exciting and uplifting, it was scary. After all, who was I to be all the things I imagined that I could be? Who was I to have a noticeable impact in the world? I was a girl from a tiny town in northern Minnesota, population 500, who wasn't even important enough to merit attention and care from her own father.

Yes, that was how I saw myself. And so, it makes perfect sense that, in that moment when John offered me a choice to become more of me or to shrink back into safety, I would choose my default. Small and accommodating was who I had always been expected to be—not only as a person, but as a woman.

I'd become a successful person with a great degree and excellent job, friends, and her own home. I never was the person that was modeled to me—a nice, quiet Minnesota girl who needed a man to survive in life and who didn't have needs or desires of her own. Yet in that moment with John, I chose to go back—to marry someone like my father and walk myself into the life that was predicted for me. The vision of myself I had glimpsed through my personal growth was too much for me to hold at that moment. (Also, the full me is gay, but we'll get to that part later!)

So, I went back. I crawled to safety.

And I'm so glad that I did.

In the time it took me to choose myself and leave that marriage (which was also the time that my stepfather was dying), I healed *so much*. I was able to shift from Default Energy to Sourced Energy. That's why I know my journey with John was a Sourced Experience.

My story is an example of a Sourced Experience that happens "out there" in life, unlooked for—as opposed to the ones I create and lead in my company. The program containers I offer are designed to shift a person's energy from Default to Sourced much more efficiently than marriage and divorce! However, sometimes events unfold in life as an invitation for us to heal old wounds, step into new energy, and become more of who we came here to be.

The aspects of healing I experienced over the course of my marriage and divorce were many.

- I got to dance a first dance with my stepdad at my wedding, less than a year before he died. During this dance, he told me I was his "firstborn," and I received love and acknowledgement from him that I never had before.

- The demise of my marriage stemmed from John's cocaine—and later, crack—addiction. I went to rehab with him, and as a result, was finally able to release the energy I was carrying about my own father's addiction. I'd always believed that I wasn't important enough for my dad to get sober, but in rehab with John I realized that his recovery journey was actually not about me. I could finally release myself, and my dad, from that story.

- By going to family group therapy during John's rehab, I learned about codependence, enabling, and healthy boundaries. That learning shapes my work in the world to this day.

- Before my mom married my stepdad, she and I had lived with several men she dated. When those relationships ended, I took on these breakups as if they were my fault. They left her, or she left them, but I'd always felt that they had really left *me*. When I left my marriage, I also left my stepson. I loved him so much, I would have taken him with me in a heartbeat—and my leaving had nothing to do with him. I could finally see that the people my mom dated had not left me either. I was able to release a big layer of abandonment energy as I experienced the situation from the other side.

- I got to make my first true *decision*. It came from within me, and it was completely *for* me. I didn't consider all the opinions or implications of others, wait for others to get better (by the way, John got kicked out of rehab), or hold back my own happiness to try to ensure someone else's. I chose from a place of power—and while the details of moving through the decision were extremely challenging, the choice itself felt amazing.

The fact is, there could not have been a better scenario to help me learn these lessons all at once and shift into my Sourced Energy. I literally couldn't have designed my personal curriculum for transformation any better! Source knew *exactly* what I needed to be able to shift my field and step into a new way of being, and it offered it through the contrast of this challenging experience.

Had I been in a Sourced Energy from the start, I would have been able to hear the information that was available in those time-stands-still moments when my intuition, my Soul, was trying to speak to me and guide me. But I couldn't. I missed it. My Default Energy pattern was entrenched, and I wasn't yet committed to letting it go. Through the experiences of being married to a drug user, I became committed and started the process of shifting my energy. The discomfort of my experience, and the desire for something different, became greater than my fear of changing the way I interacted with life. From that point on, I was ready and available to move through the core of my transformation by working my entire life, and everything that was happening in it, as a Sourced Experience.

THE ANATOMY OF A TRANSFORMATION

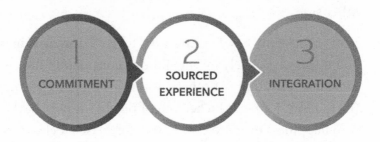

A "Sourced Experience" is a term I use to describe any experience that serves as a catalyst for transformation.

In my worldview, our whole life exists within the context of Sourced Energy; therefore, all of life truly is a *Sourced* Experience. However, the more we do this work of transformation, the easier it is to see this, and to interact with life as a Sourced adventure. Anything that unfolds, even if it isn't our preference, holds within it a seed of transformation, a reflection of our Default Energy which is ripe for a shift. Just as my marriage and divorce was a beautiful gift of clarity for me, all that we experience is part of a divine curriculum for our highest evolution.

There are two types of Sourced Experience—the *contrast*, and the *container.*

The *contrast* experience is the one that just "happens to us," like my experience with John. The *container* is the one we consciously seek out and step into—for example, a retreat or experiential program that you will create for your clients.

The Sourced Experience is the center and focal point of The Anatomy of a Transformation. It can happen with or without support. But if you can offer a Sourced Experience as part of a client's work with you, you will not only help them head off challenges at the pass and close the gap between their discomfort and desire, but also help them learn to navigate these kinds of experiences for the rest of their lives.

THE "CONTRAST" SOURCED EXPERIENCE

The Sourced Experience that occurs in the form of *contrast* usually looks like receiving a result or experience that is different from what we expected or wanted. This contrast serves as a mirror for us, and reveals the truth about the Default Energy we've been living in.

Our lives are constantly inviting us into greater knowing of ourselves and who we came here to be. Like an old-fashioned radio, our energy affects what we are "tuned into" in the world around us. Only through clear contrast can we see and recognize what we've been tuning into and unearth the Default Energy that is available to be transformed. We can then use this information to adapt and shift our energy into a more aligned state and create more joyful results.

When we aren't tuned in, or we go unconscious, we listen to what others say and adjust our expression to fit in. We don't notice the subtle signals from Source, so they get louder. The contrast and discomfort grow until we notice them—and then continue to grow until we make a commitment to do what it takes to shift them.

We aren't trained to listen to those invitations, so we often miss them. This is why life so often ends up looking like "shit hitting the fan." If we were available to listen to the whisper, we wouldn't need the shout.

When John said those fateful words, "You know, I'm a carpenter. I can help you with that," time slowed not because the moment was fated, but because Source was inviting me to catch the energetic information being exchanged between us. Had I been tuned in at the time, I would have noticed that I was being invited by him into a role I didn't want to play. But I *didn't* notice. My lack of clarity meant that I was available for being rescued, for being diminished, and for drama. I required greater contrast than what was present during that time-stop moment to be able to see the information clearly.

Over the years that followed, the contrast between what my life looked like and who my soul came here to be grew ... until I found myself changing that very same deadbolt to keep him out of my space.

None of this was bad or wrong. It was simply a choice I made. Every moment in our lives is an invitation to choose which energy we want to live in.

Oprah is quoted as saying, "Life whispers to you all the time. If you don't hear the whisper, life throws you a cotton ball. If you don't notice the cotton ball, you'll get a pebble. And if you don't catch the pebble, you get a brick."

The brick—also known as the "universal two-by-four"—can be an illness, a death, a stressful experience with a family member, a job loss, financial hardship, or a recurring experience of disempowerment, none of which, by the way, mean you've done something "wrong." Whatever the brick is, it is the perfect instrument to trigger awareness of the contrast that Source has been trying to show you and jumpstart your desire to transform.

When something like this happens, we may naturally progress through the three steps of the Sourced Experience: Release, Receive, and Rise. To be catapulted into a new energy field after the end of my marriage, I needed to move through these three steps. I Released my idea that I could control what people thought of me and making my relationship work. I Received the truth about how I'd been operating from fear of being judged and trying to follow "rules" I saw modeled growing up, and I allowed myself to Rise into a greater energy of love (of myself especially), freedom, and empowerment.

Of course, a person could respond to a Contrast Sourced Experience by going the other direction and becoming more entrenched in their default. This happens all the time—but these likely aren't the people you're working with, or that we're talking about in this book.

The good news is, the more we do this work of transformation, the easier it is to move through life without this kind of contrast showing up as our guide. Becoming Sourced means sensing the cotton ball rather than waiting for the brick. It means hearing the invitation the first time.

THE "CURATED CONTAINER" SOURCED EXPERIENCE

The second type of Sourced Experience is one that unfolds inside an intentional container for transformation.

This can happen in a program with a coach, mentor, spiritual teacher, or guide, or in an experience such as a transformational retreat. This type of Sourced Experience is what you're here to learn to deliver. (However, note that not all retreats are transformational, and not all transformations happen on retreat!)

For the past ten years, I've been offering this second type of Sourced Experience to my clients and students (although I didn't call it "Sourced" ten years ago.) As I'll share, there is a specific way to hold the space for transformation within your work, and to ask the important questions that will guide people to Shift the Field. When you do this, people will leave their work with you as a new person, in tune with their Sourced Energy.

It's been twenty years since I was first trained as a coach in my corporate job, and ever since I've been studying transformation: how it works, why it works, and how to predictably create it. What I have discovered is that the more intentional I am about cultivating this second type of Sourced Experience in my life—by hiring talented coaches and healers, joining intentional communities led by magical leaders, or going on retreat—the less apt I am to attract the "contrast" type of Sourced Experience into my world. I uncover my Default Energy and transform it without attracting drama into my life because the energy shift happens within the intentional container I've created for my personal growth.

My vision is a world in which all humans live life with an awareness of The Sourced Experience. This kind of world would see two specific shifts. First, we would hold more grace for one another when we do attract contrast experiences. Instead of judging one another, or worrying about one another, we could get excited about the opportunity to Shift the Field. Second, we would normalize the idea of getting support for our transformation by joining a community or hiring support to Shift the Field *before* that metaphorical brick hits us in the face. The more we get support in navigating our transformations, the easier it will become to see the subtle cues of contrast before they blow up into big drama.

Think about what tremendous value you could bring to your clients by creating curated Sourced Experiences! Not only could you predictably and consistently create containers for transformation, but you could also equip people to show up differently in every aspect of their lives, for the rest of their lives. How's that for a gift?

READING THE CUES

Our clients (and now yours) move through the stages I am about to teach you and come out the other side in a whole new energy. My goal is to transmit a confidence that, when your clients choose to work with you, they will *consistently* release old default energies that don't serve them and co-create new, alive, energy in partnership with Source!

You will be able to read the cues happening in their life and become a reliable guide for Shifting the Field—whether the cues show up as contrast in their life (and were the reason they sought your support to begin with), or they happened within the experiential container of support you've designed. You will know when, and how, to dive into the client's past to discover the root of their Default Energy, and when it's time to move them forward into a new, Sourced Energy. You'll have a step-by-step strategy for facilitating breakthroughs and understand *exactly* what needs to happen for them to Shift the Field.

Many coaches have excellent skills at holding a safe space, asking empowering questions, client validation, etc. These skills are super valuable. However, we are not generally taught about how to hold space *over time,* to dive deep and shift energy at its core, and to allow this energy shift to be the foundation for an entirely new realm of practical work together.

This is what we will explore as we look at the mechanics of The Sourced Experience. In the next three chapters I'll share with you the three steps of The Sourced Experience, and show you exactly how you can use them to help your clients Release, Receive, and Rise—and Shift the Field time and time again.

CHAPTER FIVE
RELEASE

*L*ori was known as the go-to problem-solver. Everyone knew they could count on her. This energy had enabled her to rise to the top role in her former company's HR department.

She loved that people felt confident in her and trusted her abilities. However, she could no longer deny the calling to serve people in a different way. She knew there were parts of her that were not being explored and satisfied in her current work, and she longed for the freedom to be fully expressed and alive.

When her company began eliminating jobs, Lori took the leap to start her own business. She'd done training as a coach, and had a natural skill set already from her work in HR. It had taken her a long time to see her own value, and so she wanted to support others to see their own greatness. In fact, she'd called her new business "Inspiring Greatness."

However, her business hadn't taken off.

While she felt more freedom than she had in her previous job, she was finding herself taking on contract gigs working as a coach, teacher, and even project manager, in other businesses. She was making money, and was grateful for that—but deep down, these choices didn't feel right. She wasn't in her full self-expression, and she knew it.

Lori had done a fair amount of her own healing work and transformation to get to the point of leaving her job. Now, she was committed to stepping into even greater freedom, which was why she decided to join me on a Sourced retreat in Northern California. She didn't know what was in the way of her freedom, but she was willing to find out.

On the first day of our retreat, I arranged for a pilgrimage guide and former client to lead us on a hike. The intention was to connect with nature—in the form of giant Redwoods and the undulating Pacific Ocean—as archetypal messengers through which Source could speak to us.

I always create an experience of some kind on retreat to help clients "catch their energy in the act," so to speak, by observing how they interact with the experience. And, while I often sense in advance the energy shift a person's soul is requesting, I do not have control over how it gets delivered.

Lori's energy shift started that morning in December. We woke up to clouds and rain. Our limo picked us up after breakfast; we would have all morning to explore the forest and beach.

We were excited ... and wet.

As we began our hike in gorgeous Muir Woods, we quickly realized that we were embarking on an adventure. While we had planned for a bit of exertion to see the lesser-traveled parts of the park, I had arranged our route so that we would be walking primarily downhill. In the pouring rain, this meant treacherous mud and uncertain footing on the slippery rocks and roots.

Our guide recommended that people hike together, and even hold hands to help one another along. But either Lori missed that last part, or her Default Energy didn't want her to hear it. She set off as a lone wolf.

Then, we saw the blood.

Lori was quietly leaving a trail of it as it dripped from her hand. She'd slipped and grabbed a branch for support—which turned out to be covered in thorns. Her gash was quite large and painful, but she'd kept it to herself and kept hiking until someone noticed her injury.

Our pilgrimage guide had brought along a small first aid kit. She provided Lori with every Band-Aid available, but since the rain prevented solid adhesion, that wasn't enough.

As she held her arm above her head to slow the bleeding, Lori was faced with something she hadn't fully had to deal with before. She needed support—and support was available, in the form of all the other women who were there to lend a hand, an arm, or a pile of Band-Aids.

Quickly, Lori was able to see that she'd approached her hike as she'd approached her business: as a lone wolf. She needed to be in control, be reliable (meaning, not inconvenience anyone by needing anything), do everything herself, and not ever share what was really happening or what she was really feeling.

This control pattern had led her to take projects in her business that allowed her to stay in control. She always knew exactly what she needed, exactly how she would help, and exactly how much she would get paid. She didn't have to step fully into the vulnerability and uncertainty of offering her true gifts as a coach and spiritual guide. She didn't have to fully look behind her own curtain.

On the face of it, what happened on our hike may have seemed like a disaster. (What retreat leader wants a bleeding client?) But it was actually the perfect experience for Lori to Release the Default Energy that had been holding her back.

This release was the first step to Lori's transformation, and it's the first step in any Sourced Experience.

RELEASING WHAT IS

THE ANATOMY OF A TRANSFORMATION

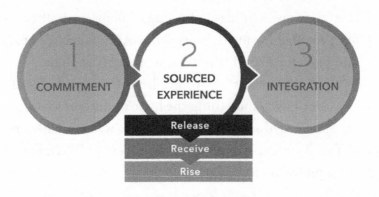

The first step in any Sourced Experience is Release.

For years I referred to this energy as "surrender." However, I realized that any time I described surrender, I was really referring to a *release of control*—or, more specifically, our perception of control.

When we live in our Default Energy, we have a pretty good idea that we are going to continue to get the results we've always gotten. It's comfortable. On the surface, that makes no sense—we want something better after all—but there is a benefit to clinging to our old patterns.

We know exactly how the world will respond to us when we're in our default. When we know what's coming, we feel like we're in control. However, to get a different result, we must release that certainty. As we've learned, this is only possible when we see, through contrast, that transformation is necessary to get what we desire.

Control is a strange and subtle thing. It shows up in all kinds of sneaky ways, often disguised as self-identity—that inner narrative of "who I am."

For example, if you want to change your self-talk but gained popularity through your self-depreciating humor, you will feel out of control if you can no longer be "the funny one"—even if being funny came at your own expense. If you created a sense of self-value by always having the best information, you will feel out of control if you don't have the answer. If, like Lori, you avoided being disappointed by people by never asking or expecting them to support you, you will feel out of control when you ask for help or need to rely on someone.

So much of our Default Energy relies on *who we have been.* Because of that, to surrender our control can feel … well … out of control! But when things get uncomfortable, it's vital to remember what we're really doing: *releasing our attachment to our Default Energy pattern.*

When we move into a Sourced Experience, our soul says, "I am willing to let go of the way I've always interacted with a situation like this (or with life in general), because I am now aware that my old patterns aren't working to get me the results I desire."

Just like Brittany in Chapter One needed to release her attachment to being a helper in the background, Lori needed to release her commitment to staying in control as the lone wolf.

When she did release control, a beautiful thing happened. She was not only able to share her vulnerability around hiking downhill through a wet forest with only one hand for balance, but she was also able to get vulnerable with the group about how she had been feeling in her life, specifically with regard to her marriage.

Lori had known for some time that she wasn't happy with her husband, yet she hadn't really been completely honest with herself about it. Admitting how she felt would make her vulnerable; if she opened that can of worms, she would not be able to put a lid on it. Instead, she'd kept herself busy at work. Because her home scenario wasn't terrible—no emotional or physical abuse—Lori felt that she didn't have a real reason to leave.

However, this avoidance was affecting her business. She'd dedicated her business to helping other women discover their greatness and create lives of freedom. But she couldn't do this in full integrity if she hadn't yet done the same for herself.

It wasn't that Lori and her husband didn't like and care for one another. They truly did. But Lori had been growing and transforming rapidly in recent years, while he had stayed the same. But her business was called Inspiring Greatness, and she knew she needed to be in her own greatness to power it—her Sourced Expression. And the power, harmony, and glow of that expression was no longer a match for her husband's energy.

Because she couldn't express that part of herself with him, she'd been dimming it. She wasn't owning her greatness, and she didn't feel free to be fully herself, which made it hard to show up energetically as that person in her business. This led directly to her contract work behind the scenes, getting things done for other businesses.

I want to be clear: *none* of this was bad or wrong. Lori had found a great strategy to get out of her corporate job and make money in a new field without releasing control. Many of us bring our Default Energy into our new thing because it feels safer. (In fact, most of the people I work with in my business come to me in Lori's situation: trying to change their lives without Shifting the Field first!)

As soon as Lori got committed to closing this gap, she stepped right into a situation—our retreat—that invited her to release control and allow her truth to appear. The afternoon after our hike, Lori shared with our group that she was now willing to look at her marriage with our support. She had opened herself up to the potential of something new being birthed.

After the retreat ended, Lori had several challenging but needed conversations with her husband. They filed for divorce, sold their house, and parted amicably. Now, Lori is living in Arizona, in a place that had been calling to her soul for years! She also developed an inspired system in her business to help her one-on-one clients find their "essence," and has been receiving rave reviews.

ARE YOU WILLING TO RELEASE?

The cool thing is, once we are in commitment to our own transformation, the Release will come easily.

Before commitment, Release feels like a monumental risk—something we couldn't possibly do. But once we get committed, the Universe provides us with perfect opportunities to surrender! Just like Lori, you will receive the perfect circumstance to practice your Release and boldly embrace the unknown.

My book coach refers to this release as "hitting the wall." For me, it often shows up like "shit hitting the fan." A Release experience can feel terrible in the moment but is never ultimately bad—even when it lands you in jail. (You'll have to scour my YouTube channel for that story!)

Your Release experience is designed by Source, just for you. If you don't understand The Anatomy of a Transformation, and gather great support, you may let the experience stop you, or even push you deeper into your Default Energy. Remember,

Release never feels safe and cozy—but when you understand the gift that it's offering you, you will see and embrace it for what it is: a great revealer of truth.

(It's worth noting that Release doesn't always involve shit hitting the fan, or bloody injuries, or a night in jail. We may have amazing, unexpected abundance flow into our world, or meet our soulmate at a totally inconvenient time!)

I'd love to tell you that I have hundreds of ideas and tools for helping yourself and your clients release control—but I don't. Why? Because we will only release when we are committed, and our Release is so specific to us that it can't be premeditated. However, that doesn't mean we can't predict that it will happen. Whenever we are open to something new, and are willing to let go of our old, fixed views, we will bravely step into that out-of-control world of Release which prepares us for the next phase of transformation.

As a coach or retreat leader, you can make room for Release by creating a safe space of non-judgment. This is critical, because in the next step we are going into the space where we can Receive our previously hidden truths.

Lori felt it was safe to show up vulnerably on our hike in part because she had no choice—she'd already bled through all her tissues—but also because we'd spent the first day of our retreat creating a safe space of non-judgment. Unlike the Release itself, this can be done strategically and predictably. In our retreat and certification programs, we show coaches and retreat leaders how to do this with ease so they can hold space for the Release in whatever form it takes.

RELEASE YOUR CONTROL, NOT YOUR POWER

I often speak about power—what it is, and what it isn't.

Many people speak of control as synonymous with power. Our traditional, more masculine/patriarchal ideas of power have to do with "power over," which translates to power as a method of control over others. However, I've never resonated with that idea. Like everyone else, I've had to grapple with my own ego-based desires for that kind of "power" energy, and I've realized that it's unhealthy, toxic—and frankly, unnecessary.

At this point in my life and business, my definition of power is totally different. To me, power is *being free to be your authentic self, speak your core Truth, and receive what comes.*

Can you see? True power is exactly the *opposite* of control!

When we are willing to be fully ourselves and receive what comes, we don't actually have control over what comes. Instead, we are willing to release control in favor of our own authentic expression.

Can you imagine the freedom, joy, adaptability, and peace this kind of power can offer you and your clients?

Most people hesitate to release control in favor of self-expression because *receiving what comes* feels scary. They think what comes will be bad, or that they won't be able to handle it. This is why only a person with internal fortitude (power) who is connected (or is willing to become connected) with Sourced Energy can go there.

The most incredible part? On the other side of Shifting the Field, none of this feels scary at all.

Time and again, with clients and in my own life, I've seen that "what comes" is often delightful! And when the shit does hit the fan ... well, it always leads to a higher-energy outcome in the long run. Always.

To transform, your client must release control, but they never have to give away their power. They simply need to let go of the idea that the way they've always been doing things is the way they need to keep doing things. They need to be willing to see the gap and choose something new.

The surrender involved in Release isn't about throwing up our hands and becoming a victim to whatever has overpowered us. Instead, it's about stepping aside to make way for Source, and powerfully choosing to explore a new Truth. This form of surrender is grounded, courageous, and extremely empowering.

In the world of coaching, there seems to be a lot of confusion around this. "Surrender" often seems to mean "step aside and make way for the expert"—with the expert being the coach who has experience and expertise the client does not. There are plenty of people who are willing to throw their hands in the air and give coaches their power, but this kind of deference won't create transformation.

Deep down, your clients know that there is something they're not seeing about their situation, and that that blind spot is keeping them stuck. They also know that they will likely need support to see and resolve it—often from a coach, mentor, or other trusted guide, or from a direct line to Source. Because they know that they won't be able to see what is needed to free themselves, it's tempting to turn their power over to their guide, rather than simply asking for support to release control. However, while this may work in the short term, it will only ever create transitory results.

If a mentor, coach, or guru asks you to ignore your Truth in favor of theirs, they are asking you to surrender your power. In the long term, this strategy will break down, as it is driven by your Default Energy. Your most powerful results will *always* come from you being fully yourself and trusting your Truth.

This holds true for your clients as well. They wouldn't be seeing transformation if they already knew their Truth—which is why seekers make great targets for codependent relationships that disguise themselves as coaching. However, *real* coaching relies on the inner wisdom of the client first and foremost. They never need to give up their power. They simply need to release, then explore with guidance, the control and attachment to Default Energy that is blocking their view.

The Release step is your client saying, "I know there is something I am not seeing, and I am willing to see it." This is about *their view of themselves and/or the world*, not some external system, process, or idea.

WHAT RELEASE FEELS LIKE

When your client chooses to release their perception of control, their addiction to a false sense of safety, and their need to be right or avoid being wrong, they experience different sensations in their body.

Release will make them feel alternately light, grounded, and uncomfortable. They will experience a range of emotions: excitement, anticipation, nervousness, questioning, confusion, and a sense of evaluating whether they are going to stay safe as they venture into the unknown. They may want to go back to their default because it feels familiar—but when they are committed, they won't.

In Release, I sometimes feel a pit in my stomach, like when you get to the top of that first big hill on a roller coaster and you know you're about to go into freefall. I now see this as "nervous excitement." This is bound to bring up all sorts of feelings and sensations, but my soul knows what happens next: Receiving truth and Rising into a new way of being.

When your client registers for your program or retreat (Commitment) and they then report to you that strange things are happening in their life, and they think they might be making a mistake, this is because they have stepped into Release.

It's nice to imagine that surrender feels really wonderful, like floating on air—and sometimes it will. But it can also feel distressing. Remember, your client is releasing their old, dependable, Default Energy, but their new Sourced Energy hasn't shown up yet. Their cells are beginning the process of rearranging. Their body is preparing itself for a new energy.

Whatever happens for your client in this stage, try not to judge it too much. It's just part of the process of transformation!

When your client experiences distress after they become committed to their transformation, like Bonnie did when driving to her Airbnb, don't try to soothe or minimize them. Instead, celebrate these signs of their release. "Woo-hoo, traffic is pissing you off! What a great chance to release control!" Let them know they are normal, and that this is part of the process. Help them get curious. Ask them questions to explore how what they are experiencing may be a sign that they are releasing old patterns and stepping into their power. Let them discern what feels true.

Remember, you are not convincing them of anything. You are only helping them to trust their release long enough for them to move to the next step, Receive.

In the next chapter, we'll step into the center of The Sourced Experience, and you'll see why releasing control is so important.

Are you ready to receive some truth? Let's go.

CHAPTER SIX

RECEIVE

*I*n 2012, I had just relocated from Cincinnati, Ohio to Denver, Colorado. My business was doing well, and I was finally "location-independent." I rented a house that was *way* nicer than the old me would have let herself consider, and I was feeling good!

The only problem? I was single, and I really wanted to be in a relationship.

I'd dated a few people since my divorce, and had one multi-year relationship, but nothing stuck. Before I left Ohio, I invested $5,000 to hire a relationship coach, which definitely felt like a commitment to my own transformation. But by the end of my program with her, her conclusion was that I didn't actually want a relationship.

Based on the outcome of our sessions, it seemed my coach was right. I wasn't going on dates. I had myriad excuses for not taking action. I might *think* I wanted a relationship, but I certainly wasn't behaving as if I did.

Flash forward to my arrival in Denver. I was feeling super proud of my business accomplishments, for being able to easily pay for my beautiful home and work in my pajamas. I had also loved the process of coming to know myself more deeply as a single woman. I knew this time for me had been important, but I was now ready for companionship.

So, I hired a fabulous Feng Shui consultant to help me create energetic space in my home to welcome my future husband. She didn't tell me this until later, but as she worked, she too decided that I wasn't truly committed to inviting a man into my life.

It was true that I was busy. During the days, I would work with clients or teach classes. In the evenings, I would move from my office to the sofa (thus signaling that the workday was complete) where I would write or do administrative work. I went to the gym regularly and saw friends occasionally. I traveled to events. But for the most part, I was quite alone—and I was starting to *get present to the discomfort* of that.

Then, things started to break. Literally.

Three different pieces of jewelry broke within a week. A lightbulb exploded. My tooth broke, instigating a years-long series of pricey repairs (and spiritual lessons). Then, just before I was due to travel to Phoenix for a pair of events, I ran my car into a light pole … right outside my own garage!

That moment was a tipping point. When I hired the Feng Shui consultant at the beginning of the month, I'd committed to inviting love into my life. But the moment I crashed my car, I surrendered.

As I boarded the plane later that day, I was primed for transformation! I knew the Universe was trying to get my attention, setting me up to Release my perceived control and hear the communication that was trying to get through. It was working.

I spent several days in Phoenix working as a coach on my mentor's team, supporting his clients from the back of the room and leading a few segments of content. One of our attendees was a lesbian and a sexuality coach, and there was a fair amount of talk about sexuality in the room that weekend.

The energy in the room was amazing, and I had a great few days. But my mind kept remembering all my broken objects at home (not to mention my dented car and busted tooth), and I had this clear sense of things falling apart around me.

I also dreaded going back to my empty house.

On the final evening of our event, I had dinner with the team. I found myself seated across from my mentor. At the beginning of our week together, I'd mentioned my experience of so many things breaking. He told me that this meant I was holding suppressed anger. I'd gotten curious about this throughout the event.

During dinner, we had a casual conversation. I shared about the retreats I'd been leading in my own business and mentioned that I was interested in taking a group to Vietnam.

"Why Vietnam?" he asked. "What do you love about it?"

"The people," I replied immediately. "They're so welcoming and non-judgmental."

I didn't have a chance to explain—about how we were welcomed everywhere we went, or about Vietnam's lack of official religion and my philosophies about how this related to non-judgment—because before I could speak, my mentor asked, "What are you afraid to be judged for?"

I was totally bewildered. My mind searched for an answer.

Then, my mentor said the words that will be seared into my mind forever.

"Ever since I've known you, there's been something ..." he made an up-and-down gesture with his hand, as if pointing to an energetic wall I had no idea I'd been carrying. "You kind of have the energy of someone who's gay and doesn't know it," he said.

The look of bewilderment on my face spread.

"I'm not saying it's that," he continued, "but it's something *like* that." And then, he stood up and walked away.

I desperately searched every recess of my mind for an explanation for the energy he'd just described—*any* explanation other than my being gay. I even wondered if I was a secret sleepwalking murderer who hid bodies under my porch while I snored.

You might be thinking, "What's the big deal?" But for me, at that time, being gay felt as shameful as being a murderer.

Growing up in my tiny town of 500 people, I didn't know anyone who was "out" when I was young. Even though I'd since lived in major cities and had many gay friends, I was terrified about what this would mean for me, and about me.

And yet, I was ready to Receive a new Truth.

I knew I wanted a relationship in my life. And I was finally willing—thanks to the divine wake-up call of things breaking in my life, and my own experience of being stuck in my quest for a mate—to see what had been hidden from my view.

That scene with my mentor has become a defining moment in my life. He shared with me later that Spirit literally came through him in that instant to give me that message.

Two days after that life-changing dinner, I was on a break during another large event. I stood in a small circle of friends from my business mastermind. One of my friends in the group is gay, and as the conversation progressed, he began joking about his dating life, and how much he wished that our other friend was gay too, so they could date.

This conversation progressed into a humorous discussion about how all people are actually gay and culminated with my friend drawing a pie chart to represent all the various ways people can be in or out of the gay closet.

My friend clearly found himself hilarious, and his banter was contagious. Imagine a group of grown adults—CEOs, no less—huddled together and giggling about a friend being in the closet as if they were in fifth grade. (Note that our "denial gay" friend was as hysterical as everyone else and took the whole discussion as a compliment.)

I, however, was not laughing.

Had anybody been looking, they would have noticed the look of terror on my face, the red shine to my cheeks, and my failed attempts to disappear from the conversation. This was the *third* conversation I'd overheard about people being in, or coming out of, the closet within two days of my mentor's observation. This time—with the extensive discussion about "denial gay," I was clear this was a message for me.

I had heard the idea that Spirit communicates in threes. In fact, I had moved to Denver because, on three different occasions, I'd seen pictures of mountains which was enough to convince me to take the huge step of relocating. Three pieces of my jewelry had broken to mark the start of my Sourced Experience. And here I was again, getting three clear signals that I might fall into the category of "denial gay."

I was not thrilled about this truth being shown to me—but, for the first time, I was willing to go there.

At this point, I kept everything to myself. I didn't let my friends know how I'd reacted to that conversation. I hadn't told anyone about my exchange with my mentor at dinner three days prior. Everything felt scary and shameful. How could I not have *noticed* something like this? How could it be that my mentor had seen my energetic "wall" for years, but I'd never perceived it before now?

And, most terrifying of all: what would it mean for my life if this information were true?

I have no idea how I managed to make it through that second event. It was a speaker training, and I was graded on my one-minute talk. The whole time I was on stage (and every other moment) my ego was fighting with my soul about whether to look behind this big, gay curtain.

I was so grateful to leave this event and return home. However, I knew I couldn't let this rest. So many things had been breaking in my world, and I knew that would only continue if I didn't listen to this clear message.

On my flight home to Denver, I remembered in a flash how, just before I'd met my ex-husband, John, I'd had a fleeting thought that I was meant to be with a woman.

A fleeting thought. And yet, it was still with me after all these years.

Not long after my divorce, I'd met my friend Pat at Sitwell's, a coffee shop in Cincinnati. Pat had recently read the book *The Secret*, and knew I'd be interested in what she'd learned. She excitedly walked me through the key concepts, drawing pictures on a piece of paper to represent the idea of creating the future and having it manifest in the present.

Truth be told, I wasn't listening. I never did read the book (although I eventually watched the movie and wasn't a fan).

But as Pat shared what she'd discovered, my mind landed on a thought, amorphous yet somehow clear. *What if I'm gay?*

Pat was a lesbian, so perhaps the energy of that possibility was simply available in her presence. Whatever the reason, though, at the moment the thought floated through my mind, a feeling of peace washed over me that I'd never experienced before. I can still remember the feeling of tension leaving my body in response to that thought; it was visceral and clear.

Pat continued to speak about our powers of manifestation while my ego shoved the "gay" idea out of my mind like a bully on the elementary school playground. Surely that couldn't be the *Truth*?

But the peaceful feeling definitely had something to say.

I also revisited a second memory of having a brief crush on the boy in the visiting church choir who turned out to be a *girl*. The shame and terror inside my twelve-year-old self when

I realized the gender of my love interest reared up in my body almost instantly.

As the pieces started to click together, I threw a prayer up to the Universe. "If this is for me, Universe, I promise I will listen. But please make it abundantly clear."

Thankfully, I arrived at my home in Denver without driving into a light pole or breaking anything, and absently flipped on the TV as I unpacked. *Grey's Anatomy* was on. Before long I realized that one of the key plotlines in the episode involved a widowed woman who was critically ill. Her son was attempting to convince her to come and live with him, but for some reason she kept refusing. Everyone was perplexed until she confessed that she wasn't alone: she had a partner, a woman, whom she'd been with for many years. Her husband had known, but she'd never told her son.

Now, what are the chances of *that* specific *rerun* of *Grey's Anatomy*—the exact one I needed to see—being shown at that exact moment? I half-laughed, half-sobbed as I realized that my Truth had just been affirmed through a television show.

The message was abundantly clear. And I *received* it.

Within a week I was on a plane again, this time to Los Angeles to meet a lesbian friend of mine for support. I decided to give myself a new experience and validate this possible Truth once and for all. Yes, I kissed a girl ... and I liked it.

A few short weeks later, I braved an online dating site and met the woman who is now my wife. I finally found the perfect partner—the one I'd been calling in all along. But in order to receive her, I needed to Release my entire definition of myself in my private life and clear the slate to Receive my personal Truth in a way I'd never done before.

RECEIVE THE TRUTH

THE ANATOMY OF A TRANSFORMATION

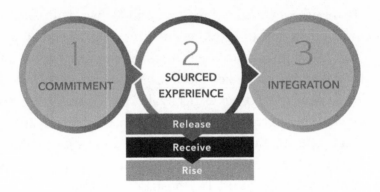

In this chapter, we'll cover Step Two of The Sourced Experience, Receive. This is the center of The Sourced Experience, smack dab in the middle of The Anatomy of a Transformation. It's the heart of Shifting the Field, and the pivot point of this work.

Receiving can often be challenging, especially for women. We are great at doing, creating, supporting, acting, and basically just making shit happen. However, after working with thousands of women in one format or another, I've seen that receiving doesn't come easily—although in theory it is *the* defining feminine trait.

The "female" part of a plug, in electronics, is the receptive side. In reproduction, we receive the "seed" into our womb to create life. Yet, ask most women to receive a compliment, or a large dose of nurturing support, and watch them squirm.

How we got here is beyond the scope of this book, but I will say that the deflection of receiving is *built into our default energies.*

Most of the women I've worked with have developed, through the parenting they received or their societal programming, a Default Energy pattern which fights with their natural capacity to receive. I'm not exempt from this, and likely neither are you.

In Chapter Five, we defined "power" as being free to be your authentic self, speak your Truth, and receive what comes. Well, it's that last part of the definition—"and *receive* what comes"— that presents the biggest challenge.

When we struggle to receive, we deny our power. Conversely, when we are willing to consistently receive what comes— even if we don't like it at first—we are in power in our lives. No one can have power over us when our receiving muscle is strong. This is a big reason why the work of transformation is so em*power*ing. Each time we move through the Anatomy and transform another layer of Default Energy into Sourced Energy, we work our receiving muscle.

And when we Release the illusion of control, we become willing to Receive the Truth.

WHAT IS "THE TRUTH," ANYWAY?

What is Truth?

Several years ago, while studying for my iPEC coaching certification, I learned the distinction between something that is true, with a small "t," and Truth, with a capital "T."

Something that is "small-t" true is something that we can believe and understand with our rational mind, based on FACTS (False Acceptance of Certain Temporary Situations). This thing is "true," for the time being, based on the information at hand. But it may not always be True.

For example, it was once "true" that the earth was flat. Most people accepted this based on the information they were given by the world around them. Eventually, with more information, it became "true" that the earth was round.

We can change what's true as we gather more information. And as long as everyone agrees to accept something as true, it remains true in that community by agreement. For example, we've all agreed to a specific calendar system across the globe, so it's true that someone who was born in a certain year is now a certain age.

Many things that are "small-t" true will remain that way and don't require our attention. But some things that are "small-t" true are not Truth.

Truth-with-a-capital-T represents what is Truth for *us*. It is personal. And it's connected to Source, our soul, and what we came here to be on this planet.

One person's Truth, for example, may be that entrepreneurship is the only way to make real change in the world. Another person's Truth may be that real change can only happen from inside large corporations that have a bigger reach and impact. Neither of these perspectives is objectively right or wrong; both are Truth for the individuals living them.

When each person lives his or her Truth, we have the best chance of creating a world that works for everybody. Those who are called to build businesses will, and those who are called to transform corporations will. Those meant to make beautiful music will do that, and those called to political transformation will give their gifts in public service. There is not one universal "right way" to live that fits everyone—and thank goodness for that!

Our personal Truth comes from Source, and thus always reflects our highest good in our journey as a soul on this planet. Owning our Truth will never take away the rights of others, only support our individual growth and expansion.

Your goal in transformational work is to help your clients discover their personal Truth. This will inevitably be different from the things they accepted as true growing up (and have continued to live by as if there were no other option). This is why everyone must Release their control before they can Receive; there is no room for Truth where old "small-t" truths still live.

TWO TRUTHS AND A LIE

When someone is in their Truth, navigating this world becomes an empowered adventure. When I owned the Truth that I was meant to date and marry a woman, everything changed for me. The wall came down and I could see myself, and others, in a new light. I felt lighter and freer, and experienced more joy almost instantly.

To hold space for your client to receive their Truth, it is important to know what you are looking for. This isn't about analyzing your client and figuring them out (although that can be tempting and is a tendency for many coaches). Instead, it's about holding space for the Truth to emerge.

To do this, we need to understand the mechanics of exposing Truth.

In this section, I will break down what it means for your clients to receive their Truth and offer a basic process for how to lead them there. Later, in Part III, we'll explore how to unlock your magic in this process, but for now, I'll keep it simple.

Remember that old party game where the players must listen to a series of statements and figure out which two are true, and which one is not? When discerning Truth we are seeking to discover *two truths and a lie.*

In every transformation, there is a "small-t" truth—an idea which isn't true at all, but rather is based on a *lie* that your client believed without knowing they were agreeing to it. The lie seemed like a fact, and thus wasn't questioned at the time it was developed. For example, "They can't do it without me" was a lie that Brittany from Chapter One believed was true based on her experiences growing up. She didn't consciously choose to behave that way; it was what she knew.

The "small-t" truth is hidden from our view until we Release our control enough to expose it. Prior to stepping into this transformation, we are committed to keeping this truth hidden, because seeing the lie can be painful and shake up our worldview. I often call this "small-t" truth a *hidden commitment*. Without even knowing it, we build our whole lives around keeping that lie in place.

And then there is the "Capital-T" Truth, a soul-aligned knowing of "what is so" for us personally. I sometimes refer to this as a "new Truth." This Truth is soul-aligned, in harmony with who you came here to be as a unique expression of Source Energy. Brittany's new Truth was that it was okay—and even empowering—for others to sort things out on their own without her help.

The new Truth often flies in the face of the "small-t" truth, which is why it can be hard to see.

The exposure of my "small-t" truths started at the dinner table with my mentor, when he asked, "What are you afraid of being judged for?" Until that moment, I hadn't even realized that I was terrified of judgment.

Sure, I'd moved through some "fear of judgment" stuff during my entrepreneurial journey, but this was something else altogether. I wasn't scared of being judged for my work anymore, but I was utterly terrified of being judged for who I was at my core.

You see, growing up in my small town, there was a *lot* of gossip. Everybody knew everybody, and I bore firsthand witness to the churning of the rumor mill. Each day, I would overhear my mother talking on the phone with one friend after another. No matter who she was talking to, the primary topic of conversation always seemed to be what someone had "done wrong" the day before. The offender could have been anyone: a neighbor, a friend, a random person at the town bar. But just as often, it was myself or one of my two siblings whose latest transgression needed to be discussed, dissected, and judged at length.

My mother was a stickler for upholding the rules she had created. She needed to see herself as pure, innocent, and beyond reproach after her messy divorce from my father (who was clearly "the bad guy"). At an early age, I'd decided that I needed to be beyond reproach as well, since her judgment of me felt like a fate worse than death. Of course, this didn't work, and she still complained about me to friends on the regular.

My "small-t" truth went something like this: "I should live a life beyond reproach."

This was a lie. That way of living isn't necessary, or even possible, for anyone. But my mother had created a world of lies around herself so she could continue to play her role as the pure, innocent victim of a bad relationship.

I don't blame her for this. She *needed* to believe those things about herself to get through that difficult time, to get her parents' support in leaving her abusive marriage, and to feel whole enough to take on the role of a single parent.

Nevertheless, following a Truth that so many people would judge—being gay—was far out of my realm of possibility while I was still living my false truth as an unnaturally "good" person.

In our dinner conversation, my mentor saw and exposed this "small-t" truth. Because I had Released my control before getting on the plane to Phoenix, I was actually open to Receive that information, and begin to open to my Truth.

Your client has a "small-t" truth that has been running the show for them since they were young, and it is based on a lie. Some examples include ideas like:

No one sees me.
I have to be smart to get love.
I am alone here.
You'll misunderstand me.
I can't show you the real me.
I'm smarter than you.
I am valued for what I do, not who I am.

Reading that list, you can likely see that these are all lies. But within the mind and heart of your client who is seeking transformation, one or more of them will absolutely feel true. Seeing and naming the "small-t" truth will help to expose the lie.

When you are facilitating this, don't get hung up on the inside mechanics of the lie. You don't even have to discover exactly when and how the lie was created. If you can focus on Shifting the Field to the energy of Truth, that is enough.

There is no one approach to bringing forth Truth. Some facilitators will have a "headier" style, while others focus on the body or emotions. This is where your personal magic comes in. I know once you understand the nature of Truth versus truth, you will design your own unique programs and safe spaces to gently peel back the layers of experience and expose the lie.

THE "CAPITAL-T" TRUTH

Our "Capital-T" Truth represents what is actually True for us, on a personal level, when we let go of the "small-t" truth we've been carrying. It generally is confrontational to, or contradicts, the "small-t" truth. For this reason, we are only able to see and Receive our Truth when we've seen and received our truth.

When I was able to see and receive the truth that I was terrified of being judged, I became open to seeing and receiving the Truth that I am gay. I had to become aware of, and receptive to, the Truth that I didn't need to live up to some random set of standards that made someone a "good person."

I had no chance of making this shift until I exposed the lie that I was treating as true. It was hidden from my view—until it wasn't.

Freeing myself from the terror of judgment allowed me to follow new lines of thinking and explore new possibilities. These statements didn't just bounce through my mind anymore; now, I could let them sink in and resonate.

"I could be gay."

"I am free to love whoever I choose."

"It is okay to make choices that people will judge."

"I am free."

THE TRUTH THAT IS HIDDEN FROM OUR VIEW

We each have a personal Truth—or more accurately, a set of Truths—that are aligned with our true nature and who we came here to be on this planet. If we live from a place of alignment with our Truth, the world works for us. There is more than enough for everybody, and each person's gifts can be valued.

So, why don't we live this way?

We often don't honor our Truth because it is hidden from our view. We aren't even aware of the "small-t" truths we've agreed to live by that eclipse our Truth. Lies like, "I need a *man* to survive in life"—another "small-t" truth modeled to me by my mother which surely didn't help my romantic quest!

Debbie Ford, in her book *The Dark Side of the Light Chasers,* speaks about this idea, using an analogy of a castle. She describes how we each are born with big, beautiful castles. Each of these castles has an infinite number of rooms, one for each of the qualities we embody in our human experience. We have rooms for joy, intellect, leadership, and various other qualities we judge as "good." We also have rooms for anger, sadness, envy, and various other qualities we judge as "bad." As we go about life, people see and notice our rooms, and judge them. They tell us which rooms are appropriate to use, and which aren't. One by one, we close off access to our rooms to avoid the judgments of others.

"Pretty soon," Ford writes, "we forget that we were ever a big, beautiful castle. We begin to believe we are nothing but a tiny shack."

We have rooms within us that are hidden from our view, and we have hidden them for our own survival. For one reason or another, it felt too risky to reveal all of who we are and what we truly want. It felt risky to live in our Truth—so we went to great lengths to hide our rooms, even from ourselves.

I'd received a clue that I was gay when I was a pre-teen and had that brief crush. I had zero experience of homosexuality growing up; no one in my area was "out," let alone "out and proud." Realizing that I was attracted to another girl—while standing in a church of all places—felt wrong to my inner "good person." The shame was immediate, so I slammed the door on that room as quickly as I'd opened it.

As an adult, I was still programmed against seeing my Truth. But in hiding it, I was living from behind a wall, cut off from others as well as myself. I was protecting and guarding a room I couldn't even acknowledge was there.

Ironically, we keep our Truth hidden because, based on cues we received growing up, we believe that bringing our Truth forward will put our connections at risk. I didn't want to lose my relationship with my mother, but I was afraid that if I told her my Truth, she would criticize me rather than love me. And it is quite possible that your parents would have, or did, reject you for your Truth. But the energetic walls we put up to stay safe are exactly what is standing between us and the true acceptance and community we crave.

It might be more comfortable to keep the doors shut on the rooms where our Truth lives, but at a soul level, we always know when we're hiding something. After doing this work for many years, I'm convinced that the very things we think we need to hide are the things that people are longing to receive from us. When we Release control, we can Receive our Truth. It comes into full light. We allow light into the shadows, into those rooms in our castle that we had previously boarded up.

This is a beautiful thing.

LEADING YOUR CLIENTS TO TRUTH

When we hit upon our Truth, it will seem as if we are viewing for the first time. But chances are we've seen it before.

I'll bet you can remember a big "a-ha" in your life that wasn't actually a new thought, but rather, a thought you were ready to see in a new light.

The biggest part of coaching and guiding a transformation is creating the context for someone to see what has been with them all along. We don't give answers; we facilitate transformation. Even when my mentor boldly suggested that I might be gay, he didn't give me an answer; he simply left me with a question which opened the door to my Truth.

There are several tools I use to help guide my clients to noticing their Truth. Sometimes I ask questions to help them understand their thoughts and emotions; other times, I prefer to focus on body awareness. While I teach specific tools for uncovering Truth in our *Sourced Leader* certification program, you do not need my tools to explore The Anatomy of a Transformation in your own work. You already hold the tools that are natural to you, alongside whatever training in various modalities you've completed. The key is to use the tools you already have to guide people through the process. (Even when we certify clients in our experiential methodology, we help them to weave their individual tools and gifts into their unique facilitation style.)

So often, coaches and facilitators feel like everything rides on leading their clients to Truth. They think, *If I can tell my client something they didn't know, they will think I'm amazing and love me and be so glad that they paid me!*

Admit it, you've been there. I have, too.

However, when you're great at helping your client find their Commitment, the rest of this process becomes easy. (You did want more ease when you picked up this book, right?) The more you trust your client to discern their own Truth, the more empowered they will be at the completion of your work together.

Leading your clients to discover their Truth involves an art and style all your own, but your process must include two basic things:

1. Being in your own Truth as a way of living, and
2. Intuitive, open-ended questions.

Being in your own Truth as a way of living means you are masterful at transformation in your own life. This is the best way to keep your energy field clean, clear, and Sourced, and bring that vibration of Truth to every client conversation. As you apply The Anatomy of a Transformation to your own life, you will naturally become attuned to your Truth, and your clients will reap the benefits.

Often, in my first meeting with a potential client, the person will immediately start telling me things they've never spoken out loud before. In my presence, people become clearer and more Truthful. This isn't because of something I do or say, but because they are matching the energy that I am committed to living in.

To be clear: I don't live "perfectly." (As I've shared in this chapter, I'm *so* done with that effort!) I fall asleep in areas of my life just like anyone—but my commitment to Truth means I will notice it pretty damn quickly and use the process you're learning in this book to shift my energy field.

The second item—asking intuitive, open-ended questions—is a great way to create space for Truth to appear with your clients. This may sound simple, and it is, but it can also be challenging. We do an exercise on one of my retreats called the "Open-Ended Questions Game" in which clients must discover the answer to something only using open-ended questions—meaning, questions that can't be answered with "yes" or "no."

It's amazing how challenging this practice is for people—including many trained coaches. Why? Because they naturally want to sound smart by guessing the right answer. "Is it X? I thought so!"

Others, out of a desire to be seen and known, insert their own stories to relate. For example, if the "client" is trying to find the answer to a story about a holiday surprise, the person asking questions may immediately begin comparing the client's story to their own favorite holiday surprise moment. However, while the questioner assumes this discussion is about the Christmas holiday, the person is instead referring to the Chinese New Year.

In guiding others to Truth, we need to be able to set ourselves aside. The focus should always be on the client and their experience of the situation, not on our perception of the client's experience.

Notice that I wrote "*intuitive,* open-ended questions." As the guide, you'll want to trust where your intuition leads you. Sometimes, you may not even understand the questions you're asking—just as my mentor didn't understand what his question over dinner would trigger for me. Remember, the more Sourced you become, the greater access to, and trust in, your intuition you will have.

Our logical mind may need ten questions and a step-by-step process to guide a client to their Truth. However, our intuition knows exactly how to side-step the process and get right to the heart of the matter.

Remember, as you get closer to your client's Truth, their Default Energy will get stronger. This means it will show itself to you, which is great. However, it will likely be very clever about how it does this! If you, as the guide, stay in your logical mind, asking one question after another in rational succession, your client's Default Energy (and their own logical mind) will take you both on a wild goose chase.

The Truth can be slippery. I know this as a coach, but I've also been that client who dodged her Truth because admitting it would put me in a vulnerable position. I've come up with plausible answers to take me away from Truth in many areas, including my weight and my level of success (both of which I eventually grappled with and transformed). I've been afraid to say that I was afraid, or that I didn't know what I was afraid of.

It's always going to be vulnerable to see something that we've never seen—especially in front of a witness. Our ego knows that, once it has been seen and witnessed, our Truth can't be shoved back behind that solid, reassuring door.

No matter how many times you've transformed your own old energies, or how experienced you are as a healer of others, the revelation of your client's Truth should be held with total love and compassion. Even for a professional, this experience will feel as tender as it did the first time.

In some ways it may seem easier to work with experienced clients because they "get it," but you will actually need to hold a firmer container because the layers they are working to transform are deeper. The fact that they are further along in their journey means it will feel even *more* vulnerable for them to look behind the curtain. They'll say things like, "How can I still have this stuff going on?" or "I dealt with this one ages ago!"

Bringing your intuitive knowing to open-ended questions is a gift. If someone you are working with responds logically along one path, but you sense the energy shift is happening in another area, trust that sense. Trust the energy. Trust your intuition. Trust that everything is Sourced, and ask the other question. Remember, though: your intuition won't speak to you if you are trying to sound smart, trying to figure someone out, or otherwise holding a contracted energy yourself. If you're in your Default, you aren't holding space for their Truth. However, if you're standing in your own Sourced Energy, your inner guidance will be right there by your side.

THE REVEALING OF TRUTH IN AN EXAMPLE

Jo wasn't new to the concept of transformation. But she was having a challenge in her marriage, and she wasn't sure how to handle it.

A man other than her husband was catching her attention, and she felt a lot of self-judgment around those feelings. Her husband knew the person she had feelings for, which only heightened the shame.

As a transformational guide, it's not your job to judge the situation, or even have an opinion about it, although you may have an intuition. For example, it wasn't my job to insert my feelings about the rightness or wrongness of Jo's emotional affair. (On a side note, if you've ever been cheated on, you need to be damned sure to clear your own experience of that energy so you don't bring it to your clients in similar situations. In other words: hire a coach!)

I make it a practice to withhold any thoughts at all about my client's situation until I have helped to discern the energies behind it—meaning, the "small-t" truth. Whenever something creates conflict or an experience of contrast for your client, *it's because there's a "small-t" truth, based on a lie, that is coming up to be transformed.*

I can't overstate the importance of this. When you internalize this information, you will always see contrast as a Sourced Experience intended to help your client Shift the Field.

I knew that, once aligned with a Sourced Energy field, Jo would know what this contrast meant, and what to do.

As a reminder, *contrast* is any experience that is clearly energetically different than the result someone had hoped to get. It's a key component of The Sourced Experience that makes us willing to see the Truth.

So, when Jo shared that she was having feelings for a person she wasn't married to, I was able to stop myself from assigning any kind of meaning to the situation. I didn't assume that it meant her marriage should end, or that her husband was a bad guy, or that the other man was a bad guy.

Until I knew what "small-t" truth was coming up for transformation, I literally had no idea what energy Jo was meant to leave behind, or what Truth she was meant to move toward. Even if I had intuition about it, I still needed Jo to discover her own truth, so there was no point in trying to figure it out before she did. If I tried, I'd only be transposing my own experience onto hers, and muddying the energetic waters.

In this instance, what Jo discovered in the process of discerning her Truth was surprising. Even though the circumstances were not at all similar, the energetics of the current situation related closely to a painful experience from her past.

When Jo was young, she'd experienced sexual abuse at the hands of someone her mother had brought into her family. She didn't tell anyone for a long time, because she assumed that telling the Truth would deeply hurt her mother and cause a major disruption in their family system. Her specific words were, "If I spoke up, all hell would break loose." In other words, she didn't want to be the one to create a mess and hurt the family.

When it was too painful to keep quiet any longer, she finally told her mother … who didn't believe her. Jo's feelings and communication were swept under the rug. Her Truth was buried.

Her mother bought her a monetary gift, intended to appease Jo's feelings, and never spoke about it again.

Of course, Jo was both confused and devastated by this. How could her mother not believe her?

Let's think about this for a moment.

Jo experienced sexual abuse. She'd worked with this trauma before and had uncovered many "small-t" patterns associated with it. However, the *specific* pattern that had come up to heal, and which now was being played out via this experience in her marriage, was, "If I speak my Truth, I'll hurt someone."

More, there was a thought that said, "My Truth is unimportant, and will be ignored."

As a result of those thoughts which began during the time of her abuse, Jo started to hide her feelings as a matter of course. By the time she was married, she'd been doing it forever. After all, why would she speak up about how she felt? In her experience, if she spoke up about what was happening for her, she would hurt someone, or they would ignore her and pretend like it didn't matter, which would hurt her.

These "small-t" truths had been running a good portion of Jo's life up until this point—but they were actually based on a lie. Jo saw that her mom put maintaining the status quo above listening to her daughter, and that her mom seemed to agree that allowing "all hell" to break loose would be a terrible thing. Her mother seemed so unfazed by Jo's tale of abuse that Jo sometimes wondered if she'd made the whole thing up—even though, at the time, she'd offered to take a lie detector test to prove her accusations.

It's often the case with abuse that we doubt our own discernment of what happened. When we are not validated in our experience, it causes us to question ourselves. This process, sometimes called "gaslighting," makes it even harder to know our Truth, since our trust in ourselves has been undermined.

So, what did this have to do with Jo's marriage and emotional affair?

Although it wasn't obvious on the surface, Jo was experiencing something she perceived would disrupt her family, and cause "all hell" to break loose if she shared it. She'd kept her feelings quiet for years, never telling anyone or acting on them. However, the discomfort of hiding her Truth was becoming unbearable. She knew she wasn't happy in her marriage, yet it felt completely unsafe to speak up and ask for what she needed. Instead, she kept her secret, and shamed herself for what she was feeling.

Once Jo could see the "small-t" truth—and the lies that had created them—she knew it was time to end this pattern. She told her husband about her feelings for their mutual friend, and shared that she was unhappy in their marriage.

Guess what happened?

Nothing.

Jo had assumed that her husband would be mad and want to leave the marriage—just as she'd assumed with her mom. But that wasn't the case.

Her husband did get mad. He asked a lot of questions, and left the house for an hour or so afterward. She'd packed a suitcase, assuming that she would be kicked out when he returned. Instead, he asked her to stay.

While in some ways Jo was relieved, this was also stressful. He wanted to maintain their relationship, but she wasn't sure if that's what *she* wanted. In many ways, this outcome was more of the same old pattern; it felt like he'd responded by sweeping her Truth under the rug, and *not* letting all hell break loose. Now, she had more time to decide what to do—but she also felt hurt, frustrated, and helpless—just like when she was a kid.

Can you see how all of her thoughts, feelings, and responses were based on that "small-t" truth from her childhood? How all the pieces of her current situation were energetically similar to what she experienced as a teen?

1. A shameful experience.
2. Hiding the Truth until it becomes unbearable.
3. Sharing the Truth.
4. Being ignored and doubting her own experience.

Jo was glad to have things out in the open, but sharing her Truth didn't shake things up in the way she'd expected.

Without the support she had created by hiring me, she likely would have allowed this experience to play out in the same way she always had—by dropping the conversation and pretending that everything was fine.

This time, though, the divine curriculum within her container for transformation allowed her to catch the old pattern in the act.

This time, she didn't drop it.

She had another conversation, and then another—with me, and then with her husband, feeling deeper into her own Truth and trusting that it was okay for her to have this Truth and own it. She had to stay clear in her commitment to be truly heard by her husband and find out if she could get what she needed in her marriage, or if she needed to leave. When she came to the conversation with the commitment to being heard—and the belief that it was possible—her husband *actually heard her*. As a result, they connected in a whole new way. This didn't magically resolve what was missing, but it did heal the old wound of having her feelings dismissed.

Outside of this specific relationship with her husband, Jo also noticed that there were many places where she wasn't owning her Truth. She began to express herself clearly and firmly on the little things, with the expectation that people would listen and care.

The "Capital-T" Truth she discovered went something like this: "I know what I want and need. I know and trust what makes me happy. I make my needs important."

At the beginning of this process, Jo wasn't able to discern whether she wished to stay in her marriage. The "small-t" truth of her mom's lie was in the way of that clarity. The thought, "If I speak my truth, someone gets hurt" was still running the show. Avoiding disruption by hiding Truth was so second nature that, before our work together, Jo couldn't see how much it was impacting her.

Jo is now approaching her marriage with a firm grasp of her Truth. She takes her time to discern what is right for her and is discovering new aspects of her own expression with each step forward. Her husband knows exactly where she is in this process; she is not hiding anything. And while she is looking forward to having a clear decision one way or the other, she is also enjoying the process of learning to be honest and received.

Most powerfully, she is receiving her Truth, and allowing the people in her life to receive *her* as a result. Anyone who can't do that is being cleared from her energy field. And whatever she decides about her marriage she will experience it with tremendous freedom.

This is transformation. It's messy. It can be hard. But it is so beautiful.

Your clients, too, will discover behavior patterns and ways of being that are no longer working for them—aka, their "small-t" truths. They will realize that these truths were based entirely on someone else's lie. And when they release the old truth, they will uncover their personal Truth, which holds Sourced Energy and is the hinge point of all true transformation.

In our next chapter we look more closely at what happens on the other side of Receiving our Truth. The Rise is where the fun begins, and where you will guide your client expertly into a whole new energy field. The three-part Sourced Experience will soon be complete!

CHAPTER SEVEN
RISE

*L*aura's new coaching business went from annual revenues of zero to $100,000 in no time.

Granted, it wasn't her first business. She'd been a top-notch independent massage therapist for some time. She prided herself on her ability to integrate various therapeutic approaches to deliver what the client actually needed. But what really set her apart was her ability to locate the pain in a client's body without them ever telling her; she allowed her powerful intuition to guide and customize every session.

Laura was also a life coach. She didn't have this awareness at first, but when addressing her clients' pain and tension she naturally asked about their lives. They felt better after a session with her, in part, because they were sharing their journeys and being validated. Then, during the session, Laura helped them tune into the messages their bodies were sending through pain, so that they could change their lives and facilitate their own healing.

When Laura became aware that she was much more than a massage therapist, she encountered a training that empowered her to name this and claim this. She realized that she could actually *charge* for this extra work she was providing, so she added coaching to her services. Eventually, she stopped offering in-person massage altogether because she was able to earn more money and have a more holistic impact on her clients' lives as a coach.

Laura now had the freedom she craved. She could travel and spend more time with her husband while still running her business. She'd met her goals! She was so excited about these changes that she wanted to help other massage therapists enjoy them too. Through a free webinar, she learned a technique for facilitating this new type of training. Soon, she launched her first offer geared toward massage therapists who'd been right where she was: trading dollars for hours, working more than her body could handle, and giving away lots of free advice. Her offer was well-received, and a whole new business was born!

It was at this point that I met Laura.

She had a great new six-figure business as a coach, with one stream of income being her specific training for massage therapists. Things were going well. And yet, she had the feeling that something was missing.

As you can probably tell, Laura is someone who has always been aware of her next thing. She came to me because she felt that her next move was to add retreats to her business model. She had quite a few clients now, and loved attending retreats herself, so this seemed like a perfect next step. Plus, now travel could become a business expense!

This was her "surface reason" for hiring me. But, as with all our clients, there was a transformation waiting to happen under the surface.

I helped Laura understand that, for her first retreat, she didn't need to take clients to an expensive resort on Maui and pay for all their amenities, because transformation can happen anywhere. We cut her expenses to a tenth of what she'd planned to spend, and she hosted her first retreat in Columbus, OH. At that event, she launched her first High-Level Program. (I write all about this approach in my first book, *Retreat and Grow Rich*). She has since created a seven-figure income from that strategy.

Her success was impressive. But what I really want to share here is the energetics of what was happening for Laura during our time together.

When she came to me, Laura had done a damn good job of implementing all the various trainings she'd done with other experts. She was rocking it in her business, and yet this feeling that something was off nagged at her.

When you work with clients from a "Transformation First" approach, the practical goals ("I want to create a retreat," "I want to earn seven figures") are *always* secondary. Yes, we kept Laura's goal in mind to continue to double her business, and then some, each year. She wanted to put an addition on her house, start a family, and fund her travel plans.

But more than that, she wanted to feel more relaxed and at peace with what she was building. She'd fallen into a habit of working all the time. She was constantly evaluating opportunities and wondering if she should be doing more. What if she created a course about this? What if she did another webinar about that? As she watched others around her succeed with different strategies, she wondered if she should be embracing these strategies too. There was always that feeling of fear lurking under the surface.

Even though Laura was making more money than she could have dreamed of as a massage therapist, she was stressed and worried about keeping up with her fellow entrepreneurs. She'd joined coaching masterminds where people talked about "10-Xing their business." She'd received advice about how to scale her own business from various people, and the different marketing strategies she should use to accomplish that.

Laura had a powerful mind. She could think through ideas and strategies quickly. With each new idea, she started mapping out the next two years of her business, and how that idea would work in alignment with what she wanted. But then, she'd lose steam or get busy, and the next idea would come through and start the process all over again. It was confusing and overwhelming.

We knew Laura didn't have trouble with follow-through. Where she was struggling was with *alignment*. Her energy was all over the place. The "something missing" in her business was missing from all the strategies she was absorbing as well—and part of her knew that this missing element was the very thing that, once she owned it, would shift her into massive growth.

This was why she *really* hired me.

THE BLOCK HOLDS THE KEY TO THE EXPANSION

When Laura described to me how she was feeling, she used the term "blocked." I'm guessing your clients will describe their experiences this way as well.

However, it's important to remember that your clients aren't actually blocked. That's just how it feels from their point of view when an old energy pattern ("small-t" truth) is running the show.

Our soul can see and feel when something more is available. But if we have an old pattern that wants to stop us from moving toward it, we will feel stalled.

When your clients experience this, they don't truly know what is going on or why they aren't moving. They sense that there is something causing them to be stuck, but they don't understand what it is. This is the wise part of them intuiting that pushing forward without looking within simply will not work!

Laura came to me to learn about retreats. But she *really* came for support in getting out of her own way. Some of this was conscious, and some unconscious. But as her guide, I knew that something was hidden from her view, and once she saw it, the insight would propel her to her practical result.

As a transformational facilitator who has magic in your DNA, this will always be true for your clients as well.

So, what exactly was hidden from Laura's view? What was keeping her in this pattern of learning other people's strategies one after the other, but never sticking with any of them?

Laura wasn't trusting herself and honoring her unique gifts.

She had built her business by following other people's formulas. She was also a kick-ass implementer. The coaches she worked with always featured her as a star student with a killer testimonial. She was the quintessential "A-plus" student.

I understood this approach. I started off much the same way in my own business, and I also had a history of working for gold stars. (I had to be "beyond reproach," remember?)

Yet to go where she needed to go, Laura would need to stop being a student, and become a leader. She would need to follow the powerful intuition that had created transformation for her massage clients and express the gifts and points of view that were uniquely hers.

In my first few months with Laura, I saw firsthand her pattern of following others' advice, then staying in her head and overthinking her strategies. She would talk me in circles about her latest plan: what she would offer, how much she would charge, how many people she would serve, and what the outcome would be. The strategy would change each week, but the energy stayed the same.

She was *in her head* figuring it out, and the energy didn't *feel good.*

I patiently watched this play out until I understood the pattern. Then, I asked for the Universe to deliver a Sourced Experience, and waited some more. (Yes, you will need to be patient in this work. And yes, you can partner with the Universe to create shifts for your clients.)

I spoke with Laura several times about how her brilliant brain and ability to map out strategies was a beautiful gift *for her clients*, but that she would not find her aligned solution from this place. She got it intellectually, but she wasn't getting it on a soul level … until the Universe stepped in.

Laura wanted to start a family, but she and her husband struggled with getting pregnant. During our time coaching together, Laura found out that, despite all the planning and strategies she had employed, she was once again not pregnant. As we processed this experience, she shared with me that, from a young age, she had always seen herself adopting. She'd had a vision of herself raising a baby with a different skin color than her own; this vision had stayed with her throughout her life.

It felt like more than just an idea. It felt like guidance.

When I asked Laura why she wasn't trying to adopt, she revealed that she wasn't sure her husband was on board. He seemed agreeable, but she wasn't sure he was being honest, and she wanted to make sure she'd exhausted all options.

Then the deeper layer unfolded.

The Truth was that she had a clear vision of the life she wanted to create. The issue was that this life included many choices that went against the grain of what was considered "responsible" in her family. From not having a "real job"—aka, working for a corporation—to travel as a lifestyle, to an interracial adoption, her desires didn't fit the culture of her family of origin. Family members had even told her, more than once, that she couldn't have a baby *and* a business.

Laura's intuition was clearly guiding her, but she was afraid to follow it because she knew she would be judged. In fact, she thought her intuition might lead her to irresponsible choices.

Just like she'd been deferring her business strategy to other "experts," she'd been deferring her "life strategy" to her family! She'd been holding back on what *she* wanted because it wasn't what they wanted for her. She recounted several decisions she'd made specifically to please them.

Finally, she remembered the moment when, after a tragic experience on one of her earlier travel adventures in which she lost two dear friends, she'd stopped trusting her own decision-making and began to think that her family probably *did* know what was best for her. This experience shook her to her core. She went home to heal, but the "small-t" truth that her wild ideas and adventures would hurt her and others became embedded. Instead, she decided, she should follow the "safe" path her family recommended.

We needed to find the "Capital-T" Truth in that moment when she'd started to believe the lie. From this place, we could finally create the business—and life—that Laura was dreaming about.

The Truth was that Laura had a massively strong intuition and knew exactly what she wanted to create. That intuition had led her to her adventures, and it was not actually wrong. It had kept *her* alive. More, what Laura was meant to birth through her business was an entire approach to helping massage therapists and other bodyworkers to trust *their* intuition. In fact, she already had a "little" teaching that she called the BodyMind Method© (which is now a copyright)—a way of teaching about intuition and the body in a way that no one else was talking about.

She loved this teaching and literally lit up when she shared about it, but she wasn't leading with it in her business because at some level she was still afraid to trust *her own* intuition. Because of that moment in her past where she'd decided her intuition had caused a bad result, she struggled to own and teach about this. This was why she would end up stuck in her head, strategizing all sorts of pathways from other people's methods and leadership; it was too scary to drop down into her body and be with the intuition that she felt would cause her pain.

When she could Receive the Truth about the past (her intuition had always been spot on), and Release the "small-t" based on the lie she'd believed (her intuition was bad and would lead her down an unacceptable and irresponsible path), she could then Rise into a whole new Sourced Energy field. In this field, she could trust her inner knowing and lead from within. She could embody fun, play, levity, and the joy of creating a business in alignment with her inner guidance.

Laura now runs the BodyMind Coaching Certification Program, where she certifies bodyworkers and coaches on how to use their own bodies as a source of intuition for their work with their clients and in their own lives.

Until she could release her own self-doubt about her intuitive gifts, she could not teach this.

Today, Laura has graduated many successful coaches and runs her location-independent dream business. More, she and her husband have adopted a baby. Her family is adjusting to her clear leadership as she demonstrates just how well she can handle a business *and* a baby. (In fact, the Universe delivered Laura's baby while she was on retreat. She shared this amazing story on my *Retreat and Grow Rich* podcast—check it out!)

THE RISE

THE ANATOMY OF A TRANSFORMATION

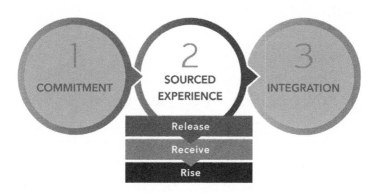

The ultimate goal of transformation is to Rise.

To Rise above your circumstances. To Rise beyond where others expected you to stop. To break through the boundaries of your Default Energy, let yourself out of the box, and step fully into a Sourced Energy field.

In today's world, the invitation to Rise is strong for people like you and me. We are being called to believe in our internal guidance and step forward in our power. When our collective ideas and strategies built on "small-t" truths begin to crumble and reveal the lies beneath, there is a strong calling for Truth. And those who are living in Truth must speak more often, and more loudly, than ever before.

At this step in The Sourced Experience, your client has Released control and Received their Truth. Now, it's time to Rise.

To Rise is not to push or fight against something from our old Default Energy. It's to create something new from a fresh, Sourced Energy. The energy from which something is created makes all the difference in how it lands in the world.

Old energy = same result. Sourced Energy = a whole new world of possibility.

In this third step of our Sourced Experience, Rise, we will:

1. *Validate the Truth*
2. *Create a new Sourced Energy*
3. *Experience the new Sourced Energy*

In this chapter, I'll show you how to gracefully guide your client to recognize and step into the new, Sourced Energy field that will create a ripple of change in every area of their life.

Are you ready?

VALIDATION CLEARS THE FIELD

In Step Two of The Sourced Experience, your client Received Truth by finally seeing with clarity the "small-t" truth that had been getting in the way of their expansion. As they say, the Truth will set you free!

But does it really?

To a certain degree, yes. Simply seeing and acknowledging your Truth is transformational. But to *truly* make space for the new energy of that Truth requires one more step: Validation.

Once the client Receives Truth, our next move as a facilitator of transformation is to validate that Truth.

Kurt Wright wrote, "As human beings, we cannot accept a part of ourselves that we have not shared with another human being and had validated, rather than violated." I first read this while in coaching school, and this idea has shaped much of my work and my own journey.

But what does it mean to be "validated"?

Our Truth is always with us. Remember, we are a unique slice of Source energy who came here to this planet to express this Truth energy in a particular way. Yet, often, our environment doesn't support that expression. Our purpose in this human life then becomes to journey back to our Truth.

When our environment doesn't support our expression, our Truth gets *violated.*

Some of us are overtly violated through violence and abuse. Others are violated through subtle rejections of their Truth-based (Sourced) expression. For example, they might be told, "You're too much. Tone it down." Or, "Why can't you be as smart as your brother?" My own Truth, "I am gay," may have been violated through the teachings of my church without me even recognizing it.

However the situation played out for us, if we are not living in alignment with our Truth, it is because at some point that Truth was violated, and that room in our "castle" was closed off. And when we tread into vulnerable territory to see something we've never seen before, we are tender, skittish, and afraid. *We expect to be violated again.*

As a coach, retreat leader, or facilitator, we can have the power to validate our clients around the very thing they've had violated in the past. When we do this, they can finally let go of that history and accept themselves for who they truly are. This is a beautiful and essential part of transformational work.

Your client will always create better results when they accept themselves fully. In fact, they will be more effortlessly and divinely guided when they can receive and believe themselves. You can call this Sourced state "loving yourself," "owning your power," or something else entirely, but I suspect it's exactly the magic you want for your clients!

When we receive and validate a client—including the part of themselves they had judged as shameful or unworthy—we show them that they are indeed worthy of this magic. They can then find the courage to show themselves out there in the world *without expecting to be violated.* This is how they create a whole new result.

I was able to validate Jo (from Chapter Six) in her experience of not being heard by her mother about the abuse that had taken place. I could say, "Yes, I witness and hear your Truth. You are not bad or wrong. It is valid for you to be upset by what happened to you, and to be upset that your mom refused to hear your Truth."

One of the reasons I love hosting retreats is that group validation is even more powerful than individual validation. When a client can share their Truth in a group, and still be received, loved, and supported by that group, deep healing can take place.

THE LANGUAGE OF VALIDATION

Depending on the modalities and methods you use to guide your clients to Truth, your validation will look different.

Validation can be done energetically, through our presence and our loving energy. However, it happens just as often through words.

Let's speak to the language of validation for a moment.

Merriam-Webster defines the word "validate" this way: *to recognize, establish, or illustrate the worthiness or legitimacy of.*

When we validate a client, we are saying, "Yes, your thoughts, ideas, and actions are and were legitimate. You are worthy."

When your client sees their Truth, your next step is always to validate.

Again, the Truth we haven't seen is often something we have hidden from ourselves because of fear or shame. Being validated says, "Hey, it makes sense that you had that fear. I get why you've been shaming yourself. But you are okay. Your thoughts, ideas, and patterns are legitimate."

Pure validation is receiving what they are recognizing and mirroring it back without adding or subtracting anything. It's a radical level of acceptance that most people have never felt before.

To illustrate this on retreat, we do a validation exercise where one person will tell a short one- to two-sentence story or experience that was emotional to them. Their partner then mirrors this back, matching the energy, without adding or subtracting. They literally say back the exact same words with the same emotion.

For example, Partner A might say, "I went to Starbucks this morning and I was soooooo happy they had sugar free coconut milk! I got a latte!" Partner B would then say, "You went to Starbucks this morning and you were soooooo happy they had sugar free coconut milk! You got a latte!" The mirroring is precise, right down to the number of "O's" in their pronunciation.

This is pure validation. When done correctly, it's amazing how the energy behind the story simply disappears into thin air.

It's also amazing how hard this is for many humans! We want to add "I understand. I've been there." Or, "I hate sugary drinks too." We want to offer insight. Some people might have a Default Energy that resists the instructions. They think, "It can't be that simple." Or, "Don't tell me what to do. I'm clever and creative, and I'll do it my way!" However, when we can simply hold space for someone else and reflect back to them their exact experience *as if it is perfectly legitimate*, we offer the most powerful gift.

While mirroring the client's exact words can work beautifully, we will generally validate by acknowledging that *the way they experienced a situation (i.e., their thoughts and feelings about it) is normal and makes perfect sense* (rather than parroting exact words). Remember, the essence of validation is matching the client's energy and tone and fully receiving their communication.

This may feel awkward to you at first, but please don't skip this vital step toward clearing out the old, Default Energy and stepping into the new. Receiving shows us our "small-t" truth, but validation releases our attachment to it.

To get you started, here are some simple phrases that you can use to validate your client:

- It makes perfect sense that [fill in the blank].

- Based on what you told me, I totally get that [reflect what they have shared].

- Based on the thought that [insert Lie here], it makes perfect sense that you would feel [insert feeling]. That would cause anyone to show up as [insert "small-t" truth] rather than as the ["Capital-T" Truth] person they really are.

- Wow, that's a totally valid response to what you are feeling!

- Anyone who experienced what you did would likely have created the same Default Energy pattern.

- That was a perfectly valid strategy for navigating that situation in the past. How smart you were!

- That approach has been highly successful for you until now, wouldn't you agree? It doesn't work for you anymore, but that doesn't mean it was wrong.

- Our thoughts create our feelings, and our feelings create our actions. Anyone who was given that thought would be feeling those feelings and behaving in this way. You are not alone!

As you read those words, you may have felt your stomach or shoulders relaxing. You no longer need to be in *fight or flight* mode when validation is present.

For many, this is a rare feeling. We are generally braced for judgment, which is why we're less than effective at creating something new. Now we can acknowledge that our experience has been valid *up until this point,* but that we don't have to continue those patterns and behavior into the future.

CREATING A NEW SOURCED ENERGY

We've come to the point in our journey in which our client will discover—or "create," as I like to say—their new, Sourced Energy.

The "Capital-T" Truth is where many people tend to stop. Have you noticed that some people have "a-ha" moments all the time but never change their lives? That's because the "a-ha" is limited. Glimpsing the "small-t" truth and the energy around it is great—but it's only through validation that we can release it. And, if we don't create a *new* energy—a Sourced Energy—to replace the Default, we leave ourselves vulnerable to the old stuff coming back in.

What we are looking for here is literally an *energy*—a way of being—rather than a thought.

It is often easy for clients to come up with new thoughts. In retreats, other participants will also want to contribute new thoughts. For example, if someone shares that they feel insecure about how they look, naturally people want to jump in and tell them that they look beautiful. "I look beautiful" is a nice new thought, but the Sourced Energy of "I *am* beautiful" must come from within, and it arises in the wake of validation.

Once you validate the client, you give the new Sourced Energy space to land. You will need to be more present than you've ever been in these moments. Your presence helps them stay present and receive the validation. There will be a point when you feel them shift their energy—when they let go of their attachment to the Default Energy. You will almost be able to see or feel it float away. Only then will it be time for them to create a new Sourced Energy that brings fresh momentum to their world.

THE MAGIC QUESTIONS

The more you work within The Anatomy of a Transformation, the easier it will be for you to discern the moment when your client's validation has landed and know that it is time to create.

To guide someone to *create* a new Sourced Energy—or, more accurately, to transmute their old Default Energy into a new form—I use what I call "The Magic Questions." Later, I'll also share the tool I developed to ensure that the new energy triggered by the Questions is actually your client's creation, rather than their *reaction* to their former "small-t" truth.

The Magic Questions are a series of queries you may use individually, in sequence, or as inspiration within your own process. These questions invite your client to generate a new way of being that is an energetic match to their Truth—who they came here to be as a soul. Sourced Energy is *an aspect of Source* that your client is meant to play with and express, whether for a season or for a lifetime.

Here are The Magic Questions. In each blank space, insert the "small-t" truth that is being released. This will help your client claim what is on the other side of the old energy.

- If _____ were no longer true, what would be possible instead?

- If you no longer had to be _____, who would you get to *be*?

- If it were no longer possible to be _____, what else would be available to you?

- If you lived on a planet where the idea of _____ didn't exist, and the inhabitants had no concept of it, what would be possible for you?

- If _____ were no longer a consideration, how would you show up to life?

You can build upon their answers with questions like this:

- What else would be available?

- What else is possible?

- Who would you get to BE in this scenario?

- What type of person is that? How would you describe them?

- What type of energy does someone like that embody?

In response to these questions, your client may give you a statement like, "I can make more money." or "People will listen to me when I speak." Your goal, however, is to get them to respond with words that describe a new *way of being*. These are feelings or energies that they can embody—and by embodying them they become energetically incompatible with the old, Default Energy.

New energies and ways of being can be expressed as adjectives or archetypes.

- Adjective examples include: expressive, loving, compassionate, powerful, big, quiet, mysterious, authentic, bold, surprising, selfish, generous, direct, alive, joyful, inviting, soulful, guided, "too much," etc.

- Archetype examples include: leader, oracle, queen, hermit, empress, follower, boss, etc.

More often than not, adjectives will come to mind, but sometimes there is an archetype that represents to your client the energy they wish to embody. What matters is that both of these are *ways of being*. They will help your client discern the energy they wish to embody in the next stage of their journey.

Note that the energy of an adjective or archetype may be different for your client than it is for you (for example, the descriptor "too much" from the list above). In the world of Source, there are no good or bad energies, only energies expressed or suppressed. For one person, "selfish" as an energy might feel aligned with their Default, and thus not support them in creating something new—but for someone else, "selfish" may feel like a delightful new path of self-caring.

I generally ask my clients the Magic Questions in various ways to generate a list of potential Sourced Energy words. (I love a good flipchart exercise!) Then, I ask the client to choose which two or three words resonate for them the most. If we are meeting in person, I may have them circle these words on the flipchart.

These words represent the focused Sourced Energy that arises into the space that was cleared through validation and will be and feel alive. Your intuition—your magic—will sense when a word or words are Sourced for this person, versus when they are simply a "pushback" against a "small-t" truth from the past. This discernment is vital because bad word choices lead directly to bad affirmations!

BAD AFFIRMATIONS

You may be thinking, "Okay, Darla. This is a lot to go through to get a few keywords. Can't we just create some affirmations and move on?"

Well, you can, if you want to put on the Band-Aid before irrigating the wound. (Or, for a slightly less bloody analogy, if you want to cut off the top of the weed and leave the root to grow again.)

Our world is full of good advice. We tell the woman who is insecure about her appearance, "You're beautiful. Get on with it!" At times, this may be appropriate—but it's not transformation. Without real Receiving and validation, before long she'll be back to feeling insecure, because the energy of insecurity has not been transmuted in her system.

We're often encouraged, when creating affirmations, to speak into what we *want* to feel, which is the opposite of how we *do* feel. If we think, "I am not heard," and the resulting advice is to speak up, we may create an affirmation that says, "I am heard," or "People listen to me." But if, underneath that affirmation, you are still living with the "small-t" truth that you are not heard (because you have yet to expose the Lie that created it), that truth is still feeling very real to you energetically. Thus, every time you say, "People listen to me," your inner dialogue replies, "Um … No!"

Beyond that, it is possible that you created the "small-t" truth "I am not heard" to stay safe from harm in the past. In this case, the advice to speak up may end up creating a trauma response in your body because your "truth" is being violated. Now, you are pushing through a trauma response rather than transforming your fear into power. You're normalizing pushing through your body's response to fear.

How, in the middle of all this, could you ever gain access to your intuition?!?

Your client's ego would rather grab hold of a quick affirmation than expose that "small-t" truth lurking in the shadows. This speaks to why it's so important for you to understand and take them through this process.

Affirmations from Sourced Energy can be incredibly empowering and effective. However, affirmations that oppose an old belief don't "create" anything; instead, they just keep the pattern going as demonstrated by something I call the Old Tired Path.

THE OLD TIRED PATH™

The model of The Old Tired Path shows exactly why the opposite of an idea is *the exact same energy* as the idea itself. It's the flip side of the same coin.

Let's take the idea of "I am not heard." The opposite of this idea would, of course, be "I am heard." We might think that this is a great new energy for someone to come from, but it is *the same energy*.

NOT HEARD

HEARD

The Old Tired Path seems like a spectrum of energies—yet, either end will create the same result.

If we are coming from a filter of "not heard," and then we affirm, "I am heard," we are still in the exact same mode of evaluating life. Everything that comes at us in life will either be evidence that we are heard, or evidence that we are not heard. Either way, the filter is the same.

Go ahead and play with this using your own energies. Maybe your "spectrum" has to do with being selfish or generous, or loved or unloved. From this filter, all things are evidence of the same thing. We will constantly be looking to see if people are hearing us or not, loving us or not, receiving from us or not.

In this framework, *nothing else is possible.*

When you apply this with your clients, you will be able to point out many examples of people and situations in their lives that they are judging using this model. You can help them to see that, while they are on their Old Tired Path, they are not free.

Sourced Energy is outside of the Old Tired Path. Sourced Energy, in fact, has nothing to do with the path. That's why it is the key to freedom.

In our example, the Magic Question would go something like this: "If it were no longer possible for you to be either heard *or* not heard—if being heard were not the goal, and you lived on a planet where it didn't matter whether you were heard or not—what would be available instead?"

It may take a moment for your client to conceptualize their answer, because this answer will be truly of their own creation.

They might say something like, "I would just … *be.*" They will immediately recognize how much of their life force energy has been focused on being heard or avoiding being heard in order to collect evidence about their story—and that who they truly are has nothing to do with that.

"If you could just be, then what?" you may ask.

"I'd relax. I'd play. I'd create," they'll say.

"If you could relax, play, and create, what else might be possible for you?"

"I could truly express myself. I'd get to be the creative, expressive person I came here to be. I would trust that the people who need to hear me will, but I won't get attached to that. I'll just be in faith about myself."

From that statement, you now have a series of energy or "being" words to work with: Relaxed, playful, creative, expressed, creative expression, trusting, in faith, myself. How exciting! Next, you can ask the client which words inspire them most right now. Imagine that they answer, "relaxed, playful, and expressed."

Notice how "relaxed, playful, and expressed" has nothing to do with being heard. This is a victory! I diagram it like this:

See how the new energy is *not* on the Old Tired Path? It's in a whole new realm, which is a higher energy than the old pattern and is created by your client from their soul (Source). That's why I draw it floating above the path.

By the way, when your client is creating from "relaxed, playful, and expressed," they are highly likely to be heard! But they aren't attached to that nor are they judging how well they are doing at it. Being heard is simply a consequence of being in their new energy field.

With each of the clients whose stories I've shared in this book, I have gone through this process of helping to facilitate the creation of their new Sourced Energy.

Laura, from the beginning of this chapter, had to explore the truth that she'd been deferring to her family's opinion of what was possible for her ever since she had a "bad" experience around trusting her intuition. I validated how much sense this made, how challenging that time must have been, and how her experience made perfect sense to me. Then, I asked her some Magic Questions.

While her Truth was that she could rely on her intuition, her Sourced Energy had nothing to do with that. In fact, the Sourced Energy that guided the creation of her retreats and certification program was generated by her Old Tired Path about trusting/not trusting her intuition. When we did the exercises, words like "free," "expert," "happy," "light," "fun"—and, of course, "mother"—popped up. This new energy became her guide to success.

EXPERIENCE THE RISE

The next part of Rise is to guide your client to experience the new Sourced Energy—ideally as quickly as possible. Remember, we can't create something new just by thinking about it. We have to create a *way of being* around it—which means allowing ourselves to experience it.

As I sat in the coffee shop with my lesbian friend and considered the possibility that I was gay, I quickly swept the idea under the rug. I didn't give myself an *experience* of the new possibility. Years later, I made it a priority to experience kissing a girl rather quickly after the possibility showed up again—because if I didn't, I might talk myself out of it.

Even if your client's new energy is "relaxed, playful, and expressed," at first it will feel like "fear, loathing, and death," because, up until this moment, they have lived with the belief that it is unsafe to relax, play, and express themselves. However, once they give themselves this new experience, they will create new neural pathways in their brain; once these are formed, they can access them again without the same level of fear and resistance.

In retreat experiences, we can hold space for people to truly have an aligned experience on the spot.

I once attended a retreat where the facilitator, an expert transformational coach, worked with one of my fellow participants to uncover a powerful "small-t" truth which was that she had to work all the time to be accepted by her family. This had originated from the Lie that, that in order to not be like her sibling (who was not viewed as responsible), she would need to become super-responsible which resulted in her becoming a workaholic.

When asked, "What would you do if you didn't have all that pressure?" (a variation of a Magic Question), she said, "I would play."

The coach asked her to think of one way she could experience play right now. We could all see her mind go blank. She couldn't imagine playing right now; after all, she was on retreat to *work* on herself.

After being asked how she liked to play as a kid, she reported that she used to like to jump rope. Immediately, someone in the group leapt up, because she actually had a jump rope in her room.

We all watched as the rope was placed on the floor in front of the participant. Then, we waited, and waited … and waited. She saw the rope. Everything in her being wanted to play, we could feel it. But her Default Energy said, "No! It's dangerous to play! This is a time to work!" Even though there was no immediate threat of losing her family in that moment—and even though she and everyone else in the room could clearly see that there was no harm in jumping the rope—the idea of choosing to play in that moment felt like true danger to her.

After what felt like an eternity, she picked up the rope, and jumped.

The energy shift within her system was palpable. In fact, the whole room shifted. She had given herself a new experience, and she would never be the same.

Lori from Chapter Five chose to use a sharp branch for support rather than her fellow hikers. But during that hike, she saw the Truth that she could allow herself to Receive support from the other women, and that there was nothing wrong with her for needing it. The group validated her request for help with few words, but lots of unconditional energetic support.

Back in our meeting room, post-hike, she was able to share other places where she was following that Old Tired Path of being the lone wolf. She could clearly see the pattern emerging:

Bold, Free & Shining

BEING THE SUPPORTER /
IN CONTROL

BEING WEAK /
OUT OF CONTROL

She began to explore the new Sourced Energy that was available to her outside of the Old Tired Path. As a result of the Magic Questions, words like "bold, free, and shining" came through.

The following day, we had a special experience planned with my wife, Kimmi. Each of the six women on retreat had a personal photo shoot, and they were surrounded and supported energetically by all of us. Here was an opportunity for each of them to express a side of themselves that they hadn't let out under other circumstances. It was one of the most beautiful experiences I can recall.

When it was Lori's turn, something incredible happened. She let us know that she felt fully supported by us and was ready to shine. She did not hold back on her expression. She danced and moved with the music in fun and playful ways. She dressed in a denim jacket with leather fringe (not the "professional" gear she'd worn for other photo shoots), and Kimmi captured that fringe in motion.

Then, someone tossed her a shawl to play with. The energy shifted and Lori became "the bird." She was present, powerful, and soft, as if she were flying. She moved slowly and strongly with the shawl for a time, then dropped it again and spread her wings wide like an eagle's.

This photo—bold, free, and shining—looks down at her from her vision board today.

The retreat where Lori transformed was designed in alignment with the process I am teaching you in this book. The entire event was curated to reveal our attendees' "small-t" truth and seal in a new, Sourced Energy. When you know how The Anatomy of a Transformation works, you can design your own curriculum to account for it. These experiences will be predictably transformative—even if you don't know exactly what your clients will discover.

Even though I designed the retreat for this, Lori had choices every step of the way. She could have chosen to push the group away when she was injured. She could have shied away from claiming her new energy in the shoot. She could have stayed in her head or tried to look like she had it all together. But she *gave herself a new experience*—one where she could embody "bold, free, and shining" in her own beautiful way.

After that day, Lori knew, at a cellular level, that she could be that person out in the world.

CREATING AN EXPERIENCE AT HOME

If you've designed your business with a retreat element (live or virtual), it will be easy to have your clients experience their new energy on the spot. However, if you are working with clients one-on-one, or offering a group program where you deliver content, you can still guide your clients to experience their new Sourced Energy.

Simply ask them:

- What is *one thing* you (with your new Sourced Energy) can do in the next twenty-four hours?

- What *one action* can you take this week to solidify this new energy in your life?

- Look at your calendar for this week. What *one thing* will you cancel (or add) as you live fully into this new energy?

- What one conversation do you need to have now that you see yourself in this new light?

If your client can come up with their own action plan to experience the new energy, they will automatically know what is most meaningful (or scary). But overzealous types (like me) may engineer a whole to-do list, which will overwhelm them and dilute their efforts. Instead, have them pick one thing that makes them a bit nervous—not necessarily the divorce, relocation, or job change!—and report back to you as they work the muscle of this new energy. Troubleshoot what might get in the way or prevent them from giving themselves this new experience.

Ideally, there will be an accountability structure around the at-home experience. The client's ego will have reasons *not* to take the action you've identified. If the action they come up with is relatively small, they will justify that it doesn't really matter if they do it or not. For example, if a client's new energy is "nurturing," and the goal is to nurture themselves, their action may be to cancel a lunch date with a friend that got sandwiched in between other appointments, and which would require them to rush from place to place with no breathing room between commitments.

The client may justify not cancelling. They will say to themselves, "It's not that big of a deal. I'm going to go this time. Next time, I'll pay more attention to when and I how I schedule things."

This one encounter may not be a big deal, but if the client doesn't create the experience of that new, nurturing, energy in a short time after they discern the new energy, they'll lose the power of it. It really *does* matter that they take that step—even if it means angering or disappointing the friend. It is a declaration to themselves, and the friend, that they will prioritize nurturing themselves over other people's feelings. If they want to Rise, they will have to take this step sooner or later, and it will feel exponentially harder the further away they are from their breakthrough.

Without the experience step, many potential breakthroughs become more like, "that insight I had that one time." With the experience step—e.g., that one bold step of cancelling an appointment—the insight has the potential to become a life-altering shift.

THE VALIDATION PARADOX

I cannot complete this chapter without sharing something I call The Validation Paradox. This concept is key to building a healthy business with self-sufficient clients who value your contribution while staying in their own power.

As you know, a paradox is an idea that is seemingly contradictory, yet may also be true.

My entire goal is to support clients to live Sourced, which means that they trust their own inner knowing above any external ideas or advice for what is true. In other words, they are healthy humans who don't need the validation of other humans to move forward in their lives. And yet, here I am teaching you that validation is a necessary step in our transformation journey.

It feels like a head-scratcher, right?

It's not actually surprising that this should be true. Many of the most profound concepts in life are paradoxical. It's how we work within that paradox that matters.

And so, let's go back to that Kurt Wright quote: "As human beings, we cannot accept a part of ourselves that we have not shared with another human being and had validated, rather than violated."

For all humans, there is a point—often before the age of seven, when our discerning, conscious mind is not yet fully formed—that our natural self-expression is violated. If it weren't for the hurt we endure at the hands of other humans, we would not need other humans to validate these same expressions to heal. But because other humans hurt us (often unknowingly), we need other humans for our healing. We actually *need other humans* to discover that we only ever needed our own validation!

It's ironic, I know.

I have two tattoos. The first was given to me as a vision in a yoga class. I didn't know what the symbol meant, but as I worked with the designer to create it, I discovered its meaning. I got it stamped on my body the day after I left my corporate job, and it was a clear foreshadowing to my life's work.

The center is orange, which was my favorite color at the time and represents my creativity and uniqueness. The orange is surrounded by a series of interlocking spirals of various colors representing the interconnectedness of humanity—to each other, and to me. The overarching idea for me was that we, as individuals, must be in full ownership of who we are, and we must do this alone. We are responsible for our lives. Yet, we cannot exist except in relationship to others, so we cannot become who we are here to be without them.

The Validation Paradox is a very real aspect of becoming a fully actualized human. We need to become ourselves with the support of others. Along this path, we will often choose the wrong people to support us. We will create dysfunctional or codependent relationships. We will look for approval from people who can't or won't give it—or whose approval is conditional to us being who they want us to be, rather than who we are.

However, we can trust that all these times when we lacked true discernment are part of our Sourced Experience in life.

The people and experiences we attracted were guides leading us back to our Truth. Do not make them wrong—but do not fall asleep.

The world of coaching is not exempt from these codependent patterns. Many become coaches because they are seeking to fulfill their ego's need to be right, to be special, to be in control, or to have power over others. For a client who is still in their Default Energy, these unhealthy patterns may feel like a "match," and may be perpetuated throughout the coaching relationship.

I have gone through this myself. I worked with a coach for over three years before realizing that I was still in my Default Energy pattern of "beyond reproach." I was seeking her approval for everything I did, and even found myself doing things that weren't soul-aligned to gain her approval.

During this time, I was still creating external results. From the outside, it looked like the relationship was working. However, my internal experience was one of moving further and further away from my Sourced Expression. Once again, I had been more than willing to give up my power—and this coach was more than willing to take it, just like my ex-husband did when he took the drill out of my hands that day many years ago.

One day, I realized that none of my coach's clients were ever more successful than she was. Suddenly, I could see how she subtly undermined the confidence of her clients to create a sense of neediness within them—a feeling that they couldn't be successful without her. She had brilliant strategies for helping her clients make money so that she would look good—but not so much that they would threaten or surpass her. More, her most successful clients were also the most stressed and unhealthy, because they were being pushed to operate like her instead of like themselves.

This toxic experience is, unfortunately, all too common.

Don't be that coach.

Do your inner work so that you are confident coming from Source in your approach with clients. Trust *their* inner wisdom, without inserting your own need to be loved, worshipped, or validated by them.

Validation should always be in service of independence, not codependence. When you validate your clients, remember it is about legitimizing *their own* thoughts and beliefs. It is *not* about you validating their decisions and expression because you like or prefer them. Leave ample space for their expression to be different from yours. Let them discover desires that belong uniquely to them. Most of all, let them outgrow you, out-earn you, and step fully into their own glory.

RISE, SOURCED LEADER, RISE

In this chapter, we explored how you will help your client Rise into a whole new energy field. You will use validation to clear the space, guide them to create a new energy that arises from their soul via the Magic Questions, and hold the space for them to experience themselves as that new energy through experience.

This is a sacred process and should be held as such. Whether the client is leaving behind a pattern of toxic abuse, or something as seemingly simple as using the word "but" to negate their own words, the new energy field will literally change their world. When they begin to view the world from this new space, everything will unfold differently. New people who match the new energy will show up in their lives and lead them down a Sourced path of creation in the material world.

We need more people like you to work at this level. We need more people like the clients who are seeking you out to help them Rise. Together, you will create massive ripple effects across this planet. Thank you.

But once the Rise happens, your work isn't over. Once a client has experienced the new energy (and learned that they won't die if they show up differently), they are ready to go out into the world and be the new version of themselves.

This, dear reader, is where Integration begins!

CHAPTER EIGHT

INTEGRATION

Maya joined my High-Level Program after a potent awareness she had when attending one of our Retreat and Grow Rich retreats. She'd come to the retreat on a whim. She'd developed a concept for a physical product, and wasn't sure she ever wanted to host retreats, but she knew she wanted her product to be transformational.

During that first retreat, Maya discovered a desire to think bigger about her work—to be more authentic and alive. You see, her product idea had been a "divine download" that came through in meditation, but because she still found this communication from Spirit a bit strange, she'd been downplaying it. Even though she'd had a strong career earlier in her life, Maya wasn't seeing herself as someone whose development would change millions of lives. Instead (as I've seen with so many clients before), she was treating this as "her little business."

By the end of our retreat, however, she started to understand that the seed of her product idea contained within it a much bigger fruit—a concept that would transform lives and create a cultural revolution.

This new energy—expansive, authentic, and alive—was the reason she chose to keep working with us in our High-Level Program. She wanted to embody this energy and learn to trust her intuition as she built her business. She knew she would need support to integrate this into her life—and it was great that she chose to get it, because contrast would soon be showing up all around her.

The first of those big contrasts showed up a few months after she stepped into our container of support, while on the first of our program retreats. Through the expertly-designed flow of our retreat—which included improv training and a shamanic journey alongside core business topics—Maya was able to see another one of the Default Energy patterns that had been keeping her from owning the expansiveness of her vision.

Maya had been a "fixer."

Growing up, she'd learned that if something was going to get done right, she had to do it. If someone needed help, she must help them. And, through her filters, *most* people needed help.

This Default Energy had led her, in her first career, to experiencing burnout. Her body broke down so badly that her doctor gave her a prescription to *rest*. (As you'll see in a moment, this turned out to be a great origin story for her business!)

On retreat, this pattern showed up in our improv experience. She wanted to get it right and stepped in to help the others on her team so they could also get it right. As the retreat unfolded, she began to see how this pattern was showing up at home in several ways. She was doing all the cooking, cleaning, shopping, scheduling, housework, etc., while trying to run her business "on the side." She was also caring for her (totally healthy) adult father, who'd invited himself to move in with her when he was having financial troubles and never left. She'd never asked him to contribute.

She never asked anyone to contribute.

During our shamanic journey, Maya saw what it would look like for her to bring more of her authentic Sourced Energy—expansive, authentic, and alive—into her home life, and how that would allow her to make space for her business. She needed to ask others to contribute. She needed to carve out space for her work as if it were just as important as what her husband, kids, and father wanted and needed.

She shared with the group the following passage from her journal: "I declare to see others as capable and whole. I don't need to fix them ... Where can I improve? Put myself first."

Maya felt the love and support of her Sourced community as they witnessed her declaration that she would make this shift when she returned home. She was ready!

As so often is the case, the opportunity to lean into her integration showed up immediately. As Maya traveled home from retreat, she got a distressing phone call. Her husband had been hospitalized after a serious medical emergency. She went directly to the hospital from the airport. While it appeared that her husband was going to be okay, they were both shaken.

A medical scare like that may have been a wakeup call for some, but Maya's husband continued to work just as hard without skipping a beat. She wished she could get him to see what was happening, and how he was compounding his issues by refusing to slow down—in other words, she wanted to "fix" this for him.

Once she saw herself starting down this path, she stopped herself (and celebrated this victory in our private Facebook group to cement it in her consciousness). But then, something else happened.

Due to his condition, Maya's husband's doctor gave him strict orders not to drive. But because he had a big job, he didn't want the people at work to know what had happened. He wanted to continue going to the office each day—but because he couldn't drive, Maya began to drive him. To the office. To meetings. To appointments.

Before long, she realized she was doing it again. She was stepping in as the "fixer."

When she committed to putting herself first and seeing others as whole and capable, she hadn't been expecting *this*! But thankfully, she had a support team in her corner. And while her logical mind said that *of course* it made sense to put her business plans on hold to support her husband through this difficult time—after all, he was the breadwinner, so he was the "important" one—that small, intuitive voice within her knew better.

And now, she knew enough to allow this voice to speak.

THE ANATOMY OF A TRANSFORMATION

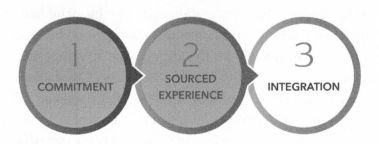

EXPECT THE UNEXPECTED

When Maya left retreat, she was in an entirely new energy field. She could see exactly how she would make herself and her work a priority in her life. She planned to ask her husband for support with their children, and to have a hard conversation with her basement-dwelling father about how he would contribute while he was living under her roof.

These actions would have been challenging enough under normal circumstances—never mind in the middle of her husband's health crisis.

After working with so many clients to integrate their transformations—and in "walking the talk" in my own life, I can say with confidence that there will always be an "unexpected." Almost every time I have shifted my energy—whether that was by discovering I was gay, coping with a team member's unexpected departure, or asking for a divorce—some unexpected circumstance has come up to offer me the choice to anchor in the new energy or revert back to my Old Tired Path.

Your client will likewise have life circumstances that show up to provide a mirror—a contrast—that allows them to powerfully choose to align with their new way of being in the world.

These moments of choice are why your client needs an expertly held container of support as they integrate this new energy and shift their way of being in the world. I'll share more details about what this container looks like in Part III, but for now understand that the container is not only helpful, but necessary to empower your client to complete The Anatomy of a Transformation.

Some people think of these contrasts (i.e., results that are different than the results we expected) as tests from the Universe to see if we will stay the course. I think of them instead as mirrors which reflect the energy we were previously carrying, and that allow us to see our new, Sourced Energy more clearly.

Without the experience of contrast, we may not be as present to our new energy and its power to create change in our lives. When circumstances line up to clearly show us our Default Energy pattern, we can more powerfully align with and integrate our new Sourced Energy pattern.

In Maya's case, it didn't take many days of playing chauffeur for her to see how easily she picked up this role without regard for her own needs. More, she saw how *everyone expected* her to step in. For the first time, she saw how she had conditioned her family to rely on her to be the "fixer" in situations like this.

It took incredible courage for Maya to set a boundary in this scenario. Surely, she reasoned, she should defer her needs just a bit longer until everything was back to "normal"? But these thoughts belonged to her Default Energy, and she knew it. If she was serious about her commitment to herself and her business, she needed to follow through.

And so, Maya gently told her husband to please order a rideshare for work the next day … and the day after that, and until the day he was once again able to drive himself. Then, with a shaking voice, she told her husband about her commitment to her business, and to being a new type of leader. She wanted his support, and for him to understand her vision.

That wasn't the last conversation the two of them would have as Maya continued to integrate her Sourced Energy of "expansive, authentic, and alive." Lots of things had to change as she allowed herself to take up more space in their household. But eventually, Maya created the expansiveness she needed to step into the role of CEO in her business and bring her powerful, spiritual energy of transformation to her own work.

A-HA'S ARE CHEAP. INTEGRATION IS PRICELESS

I attended a retreat for myself while writing this book.

The other attendees were all transformational facilitators in their own right, and we were there to move past our limits. It was a beautiful place to share ideas about our personal processes, and how to be most effective as a coach and leader (my personal obsession).

As I was sharing my takeaways from the retreat in various conversations, I found myself repeating this phrase: "A-ha's are cheap, Integration is priceless."

Ironically, this was one of my biggest a-ha's during that retreat. It was also a bit of a "bad news" insight—one of those uncomfortable "Capital-T" Truths that reframes everything and shifts the future into focus in a whole new way.

For the last ten years, I'd thought I was selling transformation. But what I was really selling was Integration. It was an important distinction.

As you know after reading this far, transformation and Integration go hand in hand within the Anatomy. However, up until this point I'd been thinking about the magical experiences of our live retreats, the places where the original "a-ha's" took place, and the moments when clients got their first glimpse of the Two Truths, as the most valuable part of my programming.

Now, I knew that those "a-ha" moments were only the beginning. And suddenly, I could see that my favorite programs in my business were, and always had been, the programs for Integration—like the High-Level Program Maya had enrolled in.

The importance of Integration wasn't news to me, but I was seeing it now with fresh eyes. The "a-ha" portion of transformation can happen in many ways, as you've seen throughout this book. In fact, since these moments of awareness are Sourced, we *never* know how they will land for our clients. They can happen in a container of support—like a retreat or coaching program—or in their day-to-day life. As clients become more adept at transformation, a shift can occur while reading a book, while in a yoga class, or through a well-timed conversation.

But *Integrating* that new awareness—and the corresponding Sourced Energy—into the client's life? That's where the juice is.

Once the client experiences the new energy (through the Rise process), they've created new neural pathways. Their ego knows they won't die by being this new way. Yet, their entire life *is still set up to keep them the same*, because it was created by an old version of them who was unaware of this new energy possibility.

While they are integrating their shift into all the various aspects of their life—and into the cellular fabric of their being—your client is sure to be challenged. Without the right support, they will almost certainly backslide.

This may not be the flashiest part of The Anatomy of a Transformation, but it's where you can provide the most value. When it comes to lasting transformation, the right support at the right time is priceless.

THE MORE, FASTER CULTURE

We are conditioned to want *more, faster*.

Look at the marketing we consume, and at the ideas and messages that drive our Western culture. If it doesn't help us get a *bigger* result, or help us get our desired result *faster*, we aren't interested. In fact, the promise behind this book is that you, and your clients, will receive more aligned results faster by focusing on transformation first!

This makes perfect sense in that human beings are designed to desire. We want to experience *more* in all areas of our lives, as this pursuit helps us to know who we are and why we're here. I want this for you, and for your clients.

That said, our culture has taken this idea in interesting directions—and our modern culture of "more, faster" will affect the transformational work you do in interesting ways.

For example, because of our cultural "more, faster" programming, your clients are likely to want to jump from "a-ha" to "a-ha" at warp speed, sucking up those hits of dopamine and surface-level manifestations without ever integrating what they've learned. When this happens, however, they will need to repeat their experiences of contrast again and again.

There is nothing wrong with this. If someone is truly on a growth journey, they will eventually integrate the new energy. But in the interest of going faster, it will often be our job as facilitators to help our clients to slow down and integrate that singularly focused energy before getting hooked into a new "a-ha."

In fact, the more "advanced" your clients are, the more you may see this. People who have experience with transformation are often the most accomplished at evading it, and having another big "a-ha" is one of the sneakiest ways to do this since on the surface it feels like another leap forward. They get excited, which in turn gets you excited. However, underneath this they're trying to avoid the challenging work of integration and move on without ever having claimed their new energy field. The seduction of new "breakthroughs" can easily keep them from doing that challenging inner work and can lull you, the coach, to sleep as you attempt to hold them accountable.

While most of my clients dramatically shift their field and integrate their new energy into their business and their life, occasionally this doesn't happen—and this kind of avoidance is usually why. Nothing is harder for me to watch than a person who jumps from one "a-ha," teacher, book, program, or modality to the next without going deep with their integration. Therefore, this is why asking your clients to commit to, and invest in, an Integration program is so important.

INTEGRATION AVOIDANCE

Why might your client want to avoid the Integration stage?

Because consistently showing up in Sourced Energy for long enough to integrate it into their daily life will be uncomfortable, scary, and at times even seriously disruptive. They will need to have hard conversations as Maya did with her husband, her children, and eventually her father. They will trade in their perceived control for true power, which will allow them to be seen in new ways but will also render them unable to predict how people respond to them. They may need to restructure their team, change jobs, leave relationships, or move across the country (or the world). They may cut their hair, up level their wardrobe, and even alter their speech patterns.

Most of all, they will need to come to terms with the fact that how they show up impacts other people.

I once had a private client who almost fired me because I went from a "sweet" shoulder-length haircut to a short, spiky one. She confided that she "didn't feel safe with me anymore." (Long story short, we worked through this and she eventually ended up chopping her own hair off!)

We can easily fall into believing that The Sourced Experience stage of the Anatomy—the "big reveal" of our Truth—is the most important part of our work. We definitely get a rush from this—it's exciting! But there's a reason Integration is its own stage in the Anatomy: it's the place where so many transformation seekers—and the facilitators who guide them—tend to fall short.

I invite you to consider your extended, intentional, often repetitive work in the phase of Integration as *the most exciting part of your journey with a client*. Get pumped about your client's choice to have an awkward conversation, give themselves a day off, or spend five minutes meditating on a Tuesday. This is where the juice is. And if you, as the holder of the container, can keep them focused on Integration (rather than the next big "a-ha" and its associated emotional payoff) you will be doing the most rewarding work imaginable.

By holding your client accountable to the way of being that they have co-created with Source, you are giving them an enormous gift. Being able to track this—and noticing when they are diverging from their true goal of *being* that Sourced Energy—is the skill set of a Sourced Leader.

LET IT TAKE TIME

I used to be in a hurry, too.

Like you, I was raised in this culture of more, faster. I wanted to "get ahead," and knew that transformation was my secret weapon to make that happen. But rather than allowing for transformation to unfold and be cemented by the Integration stage, I would race on to the next thing.

I got an emotional "hit" with each "a-ha". I shared these epiphanies in my marketing, and they always attracted new clients. And yet, at times I found myself attracting experiences that revealed the same transformational lesson again and again.

I justified this by thinking, "I'm peeling back another layer of the onion." And I did, in fact, receive a bit more information with each go-round. But the truth was, I just hadn't given myself the time and space to integrate the lesson. I hadn't done the work to get off the Old Tired Path and step into a new, Sourced Energy.

Let me be clear: this wasn't "bad" or "wrong." It was what I needed, because, as we've discovered, everything is Sourced.

However, over time I discovered that giving myself the gift of truly integrating a new energy means I will embody it more fully. I will then have that new energy as a resource for the long haul, rather than having to be reminded over and over again.

One of my coaches really helped me with this on my journey to leading with Source. The energy I was integrating was "nurture, nourish, and get physical." We spent nearly a year in this space, and the results were life changing. I was able to go back and give my inner child the level of nurturing I hadn't received as an infant. I was able to shift my lifestyle to nourish me in ways I hadn't even thought possible. I also began to explore movement and my senses in new ways through my commitment to get physical—which I had originally thought meant "don't sit behind my desk so much." By deeply integrating this energy, new aspects of my personal magic began to come online.

I began to understand that the way I create nurturing, nourishing containers for my clients is extremely valuable. When I wasn't giving the same level of nurturing to myself, the containers for my clients felt a bit fluffy and weak. However, after I integrated nurturing and nourishing myself, I was able to bring the same strength through for my clients. Next, as I explored my physical magic—the way I feel and sense energy through physical sensations in my body—I discovered that I could mirror and map a client's energy pattern, using my senses to help laser in on their Two Truths faster and more accurately than by talking alone. As a result, I added a new type of client session and shifted the overall way I was holding my work.

Had the younger me (and her ego) been leading the way here, I would likely have assessed this new "nurture, nourish, and get physical" energy through my pre-existing lens, and then assigned myself a new workout routine and meal plan while moving on to the next shiny object. Instead, by integrating these energies, I completely shifted the playing field of my life and business.

Don't be afraid to allow your clients' integration (and your own) to take time. Don't be afraid to say, "Hold up. How will you respond to *this* situation from the new energy?" Don't be afraid to intentionally slow them down and help them squeeze *all* the juice out of their current transformation before moving on to the next one. Think, "Go slow to go fast." Even though it might take time for your client to integrate and embody this new energy, every decision down the line will be expedited for them as they come from a more grounded, expansive place.

ONE CONTAINER, ONE ENERGY

I'm going to suggest that, as a transformational guide and facilitator of deep Integration, that you think of your work as "one container, one energy."

The "container" is the program you offer your clients. Whether you work with clients for a one-day engagement, a six-month engagement, or a year-long program (I do all of these), you are focused for the duration of that program on facilitating *one energy shift*. Stop attempting to do all the things in a single engagement; when you do this, you miss the potency of the singular focus.

"Nurture, nourish, and get physical" took me a full year to integrate. Maya (from the beginning of this chapter) worked with me for a year to integrate her new energy. As you will see in Part III, I design my programs to reflect the flow of The Anatomy of a Transformation and how it works in our clients' lives. When a client opts to re-sign with us and open a new container, it is generally because they have integrated the energy of their original program and have had a whole new Sourced Experience come up in their life.

"One container, one energy," is not a hard-and-fast rule as you may have clients who integrate faster, but it's a good starting point. I've found that the more I grow as a transformational leader, the more often it is true that when I hold firm support for a client's integration, that client becomes more powerful than either of us could have imagined. I've also found that each time I feel tempted to accomplish "more, faster," I find myself having to backtrack with that client to integrate their original "a-ha".

HOW TO HOLD SPACE FOR INTEGRATION

I'd love to say I can teach you everything about how to hold space for Integration, but the fact is that Integration is an art as well as a science.

As I shared earlier, their Default Energy pattern has created everything in their life up to this point. So, while that initial experience of the new energy (whether on retreat with you or in an isolated action) will give them confidence to boldly move forward, they will need to summon their courage *each and every time* they face a new situation that was created by their Default. Your role during this time is to hold them to that courage and remind them of who they are.

One of my clients, Trish, once reflected me playing that exact role for her by saying: "When I forgot who I was for a minute, you were right there to remind me, and that made all the difference."

This is Integration. It is not fancy or complicated; it is potent and clear. It is sometimes so simple that you might think, "How could this possibly be valuable?" And yet, to hold that space is the most valuable thing you can do for someone.

As a coach, the "a-ha's" feel exciting and juicy and are therefore perceived as valuable. And they are! But when the client knows that you won't leave them hanging, and that you are holding space for them to *live* their "Capital-T" Truth in their day-to-day life—that is magical.

HOLDING SPACE TAKES ENERGY, NOT TIME

At this point in the process of training my clients to develop their transformational offerings, there's a common "block" that comes up. Perhaps you're feeling it, too.

It goes something like this. "I don't have *time* to offer that level of support to everyone in my programs!"

In our culture, we're trained to operate from a "dollars per hour" space. Most of us started our work journeys at hourly-wage jobs. And so, we can tend to think of ourselves as selling our time rather than our energy in our transformational businesses.

One common way this unfolds is when coaches, consultants, and healers start selling "bundles" of sessions rather than individual ones. This has the potential to become a container of support, but it keeps the facilitator stuck in the time-for-money paradigm—often at a discounted rate for those multiple sessions!

When you are holding space for a client's integration, it is actually the time *between* sessions that is the most potent and important. You are not just offering active time on calls or at the office; you are offering *an energetic space in which you are always viewing the client within their new energy paradigm.*

This doesn't mean you are working with (or thinking about) your client 24/7. It means that together you have co-created an agreement that this new energy is how they are committed to showing up, and this new energy is how you are committed to seeing them.

In their private moments, when they are deciding about whether to show up in Default or Sourced Energy, your client is thinking about you. They are considering their agreement with you in the container you are holding for them—and they will draw on the energy of that container to provide them the courage to show up Sourced.

Because of this, I stopped calculating for myself how many hours of client calls I was committing to when signing a new client. Instead, I thought about the number of energetic connections I was creating with my private clients. Rather than deciding how many clients I could cram into my weekly schedule, I instead decided how many clients I was available to hold space for.

Too many coaches cram in as many clients as possible and lose the ability to track each client's transformation. Alternatively, they think that to offer more value and raise their prices that they need to add more live coaching time, group calls, or retreats. Sometimes you *will* want to add a strategic touchpoint to help further the Integration—but more often it's not live time that adds value to your container. Rather, it's more focused attention and intention around what, specifically, you are holding that space *for.*

When your client is at a decision point, a well-timed reflection question that reminds them of who they are can be worth their entire investment for your program.

ENERGY AND THE SPACE BETWEEN US

There is an energetic space between us and every other human being we encounter. What happens in the space between us determines who we get to "be" with that person.

We get to decide what we put in that space. If we don't actively choose what goes into it, it will be filled anyway—either by our Default Energy, or by whatever the other person decides to put in there.

In our long-standing relationships, people have a habitual way of viewing us. Even if we've changed, they put the same old energy in the space between. For example, your siblings may still expect you to be "the timid one." Your ex-boss may still expect you to be late all the time. Your partner may still expect you to be the "fixer."

Or, to use an example from my own life, your best childhood friend may still expect—and actively encourage—you to be straight.

When you Shift the Field in your life and step into Integration, you are demanding that something new be put in the space between you and the people in your life. This is one reason why I love retreats; it's sometimes easier to do this with strangers because nothing from your prior life exists in the space! (If you want to learn more, I wrote about this in depth in *Retreat and Grow Rich*.)

When your client is integrating their transformation, they are effectively changing what they put in the space in their relationships, one person or situation at a time.

This becomes infinitely easier when they know that, in their relationship with you, that space is already clear. You are seeing them as their Sourced self. They know that if they waver in one area, they can come back to, and feel into, the energy they have co-created with you in the space between you. They can trust that who they are becoming is real, and that they *do* get to be that person if they stay the course.

TRACKING YOUR CLIENT'S ENERGY

Your container with your client is first and foremost energetic. Your job is to hold that space. To do this well, you need to become a master at reading energy.

This doesn't mean that you need to become trained in Reiki or have any special gifts as an energy worker. You have your unique magic, and part of your magic includes your way of discerning whether someone is coming from Default or Sourced Energy. Whether you hear it in their voice, pick up on their word choices, observe it in their body language, feel it in your own body, see it reflected in what they are attracting into their life, or something else entirely, you will find your own way to discern whether your client is showing up as Default or Sourced.

In my certification program, I help our clients develop their own method for guiding a client's energy shift as a Sourced Experience. I also provide them with a template for tracking their client's energy during Integration. However, you can start this process now by simply keeping a file with your client's Sourced Energy words at the top as a reminder to you during each session. Using these as an energetic "barometer" will help you see where the client is doing amazingly, and where they may need some extra support.

You may also opt to give your client assignments that help them understand how they show up in different energies. This is great for group programs. For example, you may have them create a T-Chart to explore how the energy is working in their life. Ask them to draw a line down the middle of a piece of paper, creating two columns. Then, add headers to the columns that represent their Default and Sourced Energies (or whatever branded language you assign to these states).

Here are some ideas for column headers

- Old Energy | New Energy
- Old way of being | New way of being
- I used to be available for | I am now available for
- My old expectations | My new expectations
- Who I was | Who I am
- Old Rules | New Rules
- Results I have gotten | Results the future me receives
- Timid | Expressed
- Controlling | Expansive

The goal here is to help the client to see, in stark black and white, the difference they are making for themselves each day by choosing to show up in the new energy.

Following this exercise, you can ask your client to speak or journal about how you, as their guide, will be able to tell if they are in the new or old energy. You don't have to figure it out on your own! You can add to their list by reflecting back to them what you've observed about their behaviors as well. This may look like a second T-chart, titled

- Observable Behaviors in Default | Observable Behaviors when Sourced

When you co-create the energy, desired behaviors, and re-sults that the client wishes to integrate, you also create permis-sion to hold them accountable, and empower them to catch themselves when they want to revert.

Maya caught herself in the act when her instinct was to coach her husband around not pushing himself so hard. Yet, when it came time to drive him to work and back each day (and then some) she needed help to see that she was in her old energy. I was able to offer her that support because we had decided what "Sourced" and "Not Sourced" looked like for her ahead of time!

The goal is not just that your client will catch themselves in the act of their default, but that eventually the temptation to move back into that energy will no longer be present at all. That is Integration!

INTEGRATION AND FLOW STATE

When your client *becomes* the new energy, the Universe re-sponds in kind. New results begin to flow in response to their new energy.

This is the entire point of transformation: to Shift the Field to such a degree that the person experiences different results.

This new energy—which is more closely aligned with the Truth of who they are as Sourced beings—draws more aligned results to clients. They require less effort to create the same or better outcomes. They are tuned in and turned on by life, and people take notice.

For people in my programs, this often means more clients and opportunity and money coming their way. More impor-tantly, it means deep, soul-level satisfaction with who they have become, better and deeper relationships, less questioning, and more peace. They "work lighter as a lightworker" because they trust that Source is working with and through them and their clients, and they deeply value their results.

What would this flow state mean for your clients?

What kinds of amazing results could they create if they can integrate their new, Sourced Energy?

You are creating a container of support for *that* type of outcome. You are drawing toward you the client who wants to co-create *that*.

Watch this unfold over time. See that your clients *can* and *do* create the kind of flow you imagine in their lives—and trust that they will. Watch the energy shift work, again and again.

NOW, DO IT AGAIN

Once integrated, the new Sourced Energy becomes part of who we are at our core. We now have the possibility of being vibrant, wealthy, powerful, connected, intimate, vulnerable, loving, free, or anything else we can imagine even if, in the past, we may have been certain we were not those things.

Once someone integrates their new energy, they are free to access it going forward (unless they experience another trauma or violation in that area, but this is less likely once the energy is cleared). For as long as that new, Sourced Energy is "alive" for them, they will live in flow. The Universe will provide them with the match for their Sourced Energy, and they will receive it without resistance.

And then, at some point, a new "small-t" truth will arise to be cleared, and they will experience The Anatomy of a Transformation all over again.

Earlier in my own transformational journey, I used to think, "Will this be *the last time* I have to clear an old energy?" I was waiting for the end point—the so-called "Last Transformation," if you will. After that, I imagined that life would be all ease and flow forever.

Well, dear reader, that hasn't happened yet!

The human experience is one of continual growth and exploration. With each new transformation, we become more of who we came here to be.

There will come a time when the energy you (or your client) have been integrating is no longer "alive" for you. In other words, it has become so much a part of who you are that it is no longer interesting. It's not propelling you out of bed in the morning. It's not bringing joy to your days as you play in this exciting new space.

Now, it just *is*.

This is a beautiful thing because it means that it's time for another Sourced Experience! Another transformation is around the corner—and the more we move through these transformations with attention to every part of the Anatomy, the easier and more "flowy" they become. We know what is about to happen, and we understand that on the other side is freedom. So rather than resist the contrast when it shows up, we get excited, because we know we are about to be invited into a new Sourced Energy.

I believe that if we consistently work within containers of support—such as retreats and coaching programs that support transformation first—and honor the stages of the Anatomy, we will move through these experiences with great joy and delight.

If we think we are done or decide we don't want to do this whole transformation thing anymore, we will have another moment where shit hits the fan.

The Greek philosopher Heraclitus said, "The only constant is change."

We are invited, continually, to transform.

And we are likewise invited, as facilitators of transformation, to create businesses models which honor this sacred human process of growth and deliver the true, Source-guided transformation our clients crave, over and over again.

In Part III, I'll show you exactly how to design your business model to put transformation first while holding your personal gifts front and center.

PART III

INTEGRATING TRANSFORMATION IN YOUR BUSINESS

CHAPTER NINE

UNLOCK YOUR MAGIC

*B*efore you can design programs to facilitate transformation, it is extremely helpful to get clear on one very important thing:

Your personal magic.

Your magic is inside you. It's unique. Every training, certification, and life experience under your belt has played a part in honing this power. It's that thing you do so naturally that it's like breathing. It's the thing you do when you drop all the analytical thoughts and just *be* with your client (or friend, or partner, or child) in the moment. At these times, your inner knowing—your intuitive gift, or what I call your Sourced Magic—comes alive.

You can (and will) continue to develop your skills along your journey—but make no mistake, you are already fully equipped to hold the container for transformation. I've come to realize that we all have an inner knowing, guided by Source, that allows us to see, feel, and recognize Truth. Embracing the approach that I'm about to share with you in this chapter will allow you to use your gifts within The Anatomy of a Transformation. This will empower you to create the kinds of client results I've shared in this book with grace and ease, because you've got the power of your Sourced Magic working for you.

THE SIX SOURCED MAGICS

So, what is your magic, anyway?

Merriam-Webster defines magic as *the use of means believed to have supernatural powers*, or *extraordinary power of influence seemingly from a supernatural source.*

Whether your magic is supernatural or not can be debated, but in the end it doesn't really matter. What matters is what you can *do* with it.

To me, your magic has to do with the way you *see, know, transmute,* or *transform* something to create an unpredictable/non-linear shift in energy or a quantum leap in outcome.

As I shared earlier, your magic is a combination of your life experience, training, and energetic activations you've received over the years. It's like a beautiful, transformational collage! But no matter how it was shaped, your magic will predictably help you *see, know, transmute,* or *transform.* For this reason, it's linked directly to your ability to guide the transformational process for others and guide others to see, interact with, and own their own Truth.

All forms of magic have three things in common.

First, they all represent Source working through you for the greatest good and highest alignment of your individual clients.

Second, they support you in being able to track where your client is in terms of their awareness of, or ability to see, that which was previously hidden from view. In other words, your magic allows you, in some way, to *perceive what they are perceiving.*

Third, all forms of magic allow you to see, feel, or perceive what your client can't yet see. This empowers you to hold space for their Sourced Expression as they move through The Anatomy of a Transformation.

Identifying and naming your own unique magic is a process, and there are literally infinite ways your Sourced Magic can be expressed. However, over the years I've identified six archetypal forms of magic. Chances are, yours will fall into one (or more) of these broad categories. If you haven't already honed in on your magic, this can help you remove the "mystery" of your gifts enough to start deliberately using them with your clients. As you gain more experience, you will get to know your magic better.

THE SIX SOURCED MAGICS

1. Recognition
2. Compassion
3. Sensation
4. Expansion
5. Vibration
6. Expression

I've noticed that most people have one form of magic that is dominant. Perhaps you've noticed this form first because of its clear prominence in the way you live and work. This is your natural magic. However, you may recognize other forms that are less visible and which you can choose to develop further. It's also common for magical archetypes to overlap, so it's perfectly okay if you identify with more than one! Above all, we are growth-oriented beings who will continue to evolve our magic as our lives unfold.

If you don't yet consider yourself magical, I suggest reviewing the following descriptions with an eye toward selecting one area you can claim as valid, valuable, and safe to get visible within. What would be possible if you stopped holding your gifts as "strange," "weird," "or "woo-woo" and began to lead with them overtly? What fabulous, exciting people and experiences would be drawn to you?

On the other hand, if several of these feel comfortable for you, select one to practice with and continue growing into; set the intention to play with it in your work for the next few months to see what unfolds.

YOUR SOURCED MAGIC

Here are the six types of Sourced Magic. Which Magician are you? (Note: Take my Sourced Magic Quiz at www.ShiftTheField. com/resources to get a more complete description of how to expand your magic!)

THE RECOGNITION MAGICIAN

Strengths

- You see patterns in ideas, language, social trends, and more.

- You may see ten steps ahead and "just know" how something will play out in advance.

- You may get a "click" when seeing or thinking of something and know it's a message.

- You may see visual images that you recognize as an idea of the future that will come to fruition.

- When you see an opportunity, you recognize whether it is for you—even if it makes *no sense* based on who you have been. (This also works for your clients.)

- When your clients experience an obstacle, you can often see the pattern of behavior that has led to this obstacle and how to move around it.

Challenges

- Wanting to share what you know when someone isn't ready.

- Seeing so far ahead that people don't "get you" when you speak.

- Being timing-challenged. (You may launch something years before it is ready to be birthed!)

- Waiting around for "signs" because you generally need something external to respond to/recognize.

Your magic brings Truth by ...

Recognizing and naming the "small-t" truth patterns that have brought your client to where they are. You also see what new pattern, based in "Capital-T" Truth, will get them to the result they desire!

THE COMPASSION MAGICIAN

Strengths

- You love and nurture the people around you and are compassionate toward the challenges they experience.

- You know that to be loving to others, you must first bring love and compassion to yourself. Being willing to love yourself is how you've cultivated your gift to love others.

- While you may be conscious of another's "pain" and wish to alleviate it, you also see them as whole and completely capable of navigating their own experience.

- Being compassionately present with another, while seeing them wholly capable of moving through anything, is a gift that invites others to rise to the occasion.

- You sense that your work is most powerful when you keep your boundaries solid and the energy of the containers you create clean, clear, and "fixing-free."

Challenges

- Saying yes to things that will be "helpful" to someone but aren't necessarily yours to do.

- Feeling uneasy or guilty for not "putting yourself out there."

- Overthinking about people who need your work but who you don't currently serve. You may even create whole programs that are not aligned, or that you don't have the time or energy to deliver, because you think you should help.

- Forgetting to make time for your own nurturing, even though it is the key to your magic.

Your magic brings Truth by ...

Removing barriers to an individual's self-love and personal sense of empowerment. You do this by simply not believing that anything other than their full love and power is possible for them; this invites them into this belief as well! From this place, they are able to see their own truth.

THE SENSATION MAGICIAN

Strengths

- You feel things deeply, often on both a physical and emotional level.

- You may feel things that aren't yours, including others' symptoms, energy patterns, or emotions. This can help you deeply tune in to your clients.

- You are able to use all of your senses to receive information about an experience or situation—including if something "smells" off. Simply touching something to your skin may open up your knowing.

- You may connect deeply with nature in a very sensual way.

- The textures of clothing and materials are important to you.

- You need movement to be at your best. Whether hiking, dancing or traveling, you thrive on getting out from behind your laptop!

- You may relate to the idea that you are literally "moving energy" with your own body.

Challenges

- Feeling things that aren't yours but interpreting them as yours.

- Needing to clear your body/chakras regularly.

- Knowing how to package this magic as a gift (since it's not as obviously valued as other magics in our modern culture).

- Experiencing a lot of physical symptoms as signs or messages.

- Being a sensation junkie.

Your magic brings Truth by …

Sensing what the "small-t" truth feels like in your client's body or emotional field; thus, you are able to bring presence and validation to that past experience. Then, you can move the energy and free your client up to create a new Truth.

THE EXPANSION MAGICIAN

Strengths

- Abundant thoughts come naturally to you. You see a mansion where others see shacks.

- You see how to "amplify" things to make them bigger, better, and *more*.

- When your client has an idea, you will immediately know how this idea can be expanded. You always see possibility.

- You understand the *global* impact of what you are doing on a day-to-day basis.

- The Universe is your playground, and you delight in experimenting with what is possible to create in this life!

Challenges

- Frustration with small thinkers and the status quo. You don't understand why so many settle for so little.

- Making plans based on abundance thinking, only to have them impacted by those who are thinking in lack. When this happens, you may not follow through on your original vision. This will sometimes feel like a start/stop experience.

- Wanting to hoard resources/collect abundance rather than trust and recirculate.

- Wanting to make something bigger out of something that people were perfectly happy with in its original form.

- Seeing abundance for others but forgetting to apply it to yourself.

Your magic brings Truth by ...

Operating from a framework of abundance. You know that a "small-t" truth always stems from lack, while Truth always comes from a place of abundance. By refusing to see lack, you will invite your client to view a new Truth that aligns with the Universal Truth of abundance. (Note: Don't forget to validate your client's perception, even if you know a larger Truth exists!)

THE VIBRATION MAGICIAN

Strengths

- You are often described as having "good energy," and sense that people are drawn to you because of that.

- You tend to sense the vibration of a person first—the tone and energy that their body is communicating—before you even process their words.

- Your instinct is to notice how a person's vibration is in the way of what they want. You know they can transform their energy to get a different result! You weave your world with energy.

- If you find yourself feeling heavy or uninspired, you quickly remind yourself that a different vibration is possible and shift to a new energy. (You've probably done many layers of work on your own transformation to make this rapid shift possible!)

- When you interact with something—a marketing message, social media post, or product—you feel the vibration of the creator. When you put something out into the world, you always pause to check the energy of it.

Challenges

- Feeling like an alien at times. Most people don't see or work in energy, so it can get lonely in your space.

- Falling into the vibration of the people around you when you forget to be intentional.

- Feeling constant resistance from others who don't realize that they have the power to change their energy. (You may need to educate people.)

- Distrusting your vibrational knowing about something because others seem to love it.

Your magic brings Truth by ...

Helping your client see beyond the words and logic to the energy that they have been living with. Energy is a more truthful guide than words. You can discern the vibration of their "small-t" truth and get present to its impact. Then, you can support them to fiercely commit to living in a new way and inviting a vibration that aligns with their personal Truth!

THE EXPRESSION MAGICIAN

Strengths

- You allow Spirit to express through you, following what moves you in the moment without thinking about the future or the past.

- You transform people with your presence because you are so *present*.

- You are willing to say what is "up" for you, even if it makes others uncomfortable. People receive what you say because of your powerful presence and commitment to your own vulnerability.

- You may express through words, visual art, movement, sound, or some combination that is uniquely yours.

- Sometimes, you may recognize that what is coming through you is coming from *somewhere else*, not your conscious mind. Whatever your form of expression, you are a channel.

Challenges

- Avoiding planning for the future because you're so much happier in the present.

- Not knowing how your gift will show up from moment to moment, and therefore feeling unable to value it, and market it.

- Succumbing to pressure from others to conform and hold back on your expression, or to think things through before you speak. (Sometimes this may be good advice, but not usually.)

Your magic brings Truth by ...

Channeling the exact message, energy, sound, or combination of factors that your client needs in order to receive their Two Truths. Whether via divine downloads about what is True now or a spontaneous song that moves the energy, you are a vessel for the Truth to come through directly from Source. Whether you, or your client, consciously understand what happened in the moment, the transformation is complete! (Note: be sure to have a conversation afterward to help bring the new Truth to your client's conscious awareness and brainstorm the ways they can give themselves the experience of the new Sourced Energy within a few days so they can powerfully Integrate the shift you've facilitated!)

YOUR MAGIC AND THE DIVINE CURRICULUM

Which of the Six Magics did you resonate with the most? Do you see yourself in more than one—or have you evolved from using one form of magic to another?

If you don't recognize your magic directly from your client work, you may see it clearly in your life events. Maybe you made a big decision based on vibration rather than logic, and everything changed in a beautiful way. Or maybe you're the go-to person when your friends need advice, because you can easily pluck the Truth from their conversations based on the patterns in their word usage.

Your magic will always feel natural and instinctive to you. Don't be tempted to dismiss it. Not only is it unique to you and your Sourced expression in this lifetime, it's also exactly what your clients need to activate their own magic and receive transformational growth.

When your clients are in your container (aka, the "black box" I mentioned in Chapter Two), they are not only interacting with you but with their life experience. Their life provides the divine curriculum for their transformation. The Sourced Experiences that happen in their lives, and within your magical container, make for explosive growth. It's not our job as facilitators to judge, evaluate, or try to change these experiences, but rather to hold a container where any "tough" things in their life can be interpreted as part of this growth rather than "blocks" or obstacles to be overcome.

So many of my clients have moved through major losses, illnesses, or other changes that felt outside of their control while being held in my container of support. Sometimes people think "bad news" is a sign that they should not have signed up for coaching. They want to wait until they are through the hard time and then come back to get support.

We have an epidemic of lone wolf syndrome in our Western culture. At this stage in our evolution as a society, supporting someone as they move through a challenge is a radical, even revolutionary, act. And just because things are less than perfect in our lives does not mean we are unable to transform, to create, or to receive support. Much the opposite.

The divine curriculum is always right on time.

OWNING YOUR MAGIC

When I was still working my corporate job, I once got "constructive" feedback during a performance review.

"Tone down those soft skills," my supervisor told me. "They're great, but they'll only get you so far in a Fortune 20 company. Focus on your technical skills."

This feedback stuck with me for a long time. While I received high scores in that review and a promotion, that one statement made the biggest impression.

My "soft skills"—like my ability to communicate clearly with others, to get into the minds of our consumers and predict how they were likely to behave, to feel the energy of projects, and inspire team members to "carry the torch"—were my magic. My technical skills were solid, but they weren't the key to my success. I knew it then, and I know it even more deeply today.

Still, that review haunted me for years.

For many people, their technical skills *are* their magic— their strongest gifts, aligned perfectly with their life purpose and the good of the planet. I have no judgment of anyone else's magic, and I'm super grateful that all those tech geniuses followed their passions because their advancements allow me to do my work from anywhere in the world, with only a laptop!

But never, for one second, do I think that their contributions are more valuable than the magic of people like us.

In fact, the faster technology moves our society, the more critical it becomes for us to nurture and value the transformational arts. We need more support than ever to be fully human. When we're moving at lightning speed and constantly communicating via technology, it's vital for us to stay present and connected to our bodies, clear our energy fields, and actually feel our emotions.

Those of us who work in transformation know this. We feel it.

But overall, our society doesn't yet believe it.

Although "spiritual" ideas are becoming more common in media, film, and even education, they are often shared tongue-in-cheek. Spiritually driven characters are represented as unreliable, out of touch, or simply as comic relief. It's not usual to see a spiritual person portrayed as a powerful leader who is making an impact.

It's up to you, reader, to let go of any negative beliefs you may still be carrying about the value of your "soft skills." It's up to you to stop hiding the magical parts of yourself, to stop buying into the strictly rational/linear/logical (aka, masculine) ideas of what is valuable, and to stop operating according to old models of "how the world works."

Instead, boldly honor your feminine, intuitive gifts—regardless of the body you live in, where you come from, or what others have told you is possible.

We can't Receive it until we become it.

So, own your magic publicly, and become the Sourced Leader that the world needs you to be.

PUTTING YOUR MAGIC TO WORK

If you're already using your magic in your business, you may have noticed that your gifts aren't always predictable. Day by day, they may be accessible to different degrees—and sometimes, they might feel like they disappear altogether.

Your magic is not available to you when you are thinking about ten other things, analyzing how you need to show up, wondering what others are thinking about you, or plotting what to do next; it is only accessible when you are fully present. This is why having a business model that allows you to be in flow and fully present is so valuable: it allows you to Release your perceived control and surrender to the Truth that is arising to be seen, felt, and heard.

When we are in the present moment, fully embodied, we create a sacred space that allows us to bring forth our magic. We may hear things that are unspoken, or "just know" exactly what needs to happen in response to the energy of the moment. We become aware of so much *more* than what our logical mind can pick up on. (Remember, the logical mind is unable to perceive Truth!)

Making friends with your body is a critical part of the work of becoming Sourced because it allows us to get out of our heads and into our hearts. We can move into the power center of our Sacral Chakra (our gut knowing) and use all of our senses to bring Truth forward in any situation. In other words, we need to become *embodied* in our magic.

While writing this chapter, I got on a call with my brilliant book coach, Pat Verducci, who is an adjunct professor of screenwriting. She shared with me her personal experience with embodiment.

When Pat is reviewing manuscripts for her students, she is usually feeling very analytical and "in her head" with her feedback. (She writes lots of notes in the margins!) But when she comes to a workshop circle and is able to respond to the energy of the writers in the room, an entirely other set of words comes out of her mouth.

Yes, her logical mind and extensive notes help her prepare for those conversations, but each time she is aware of her magic and allows it to come forward, she sets aside those notes and instead trusts her inner knowing about what is needed.

I've experienced her magic when we are reviewing my books and tuning into what my readers need to hear. It reminds me of my own experience working with retreat leader clients as they prepare to host their first retreats.

Often, when clients come to me, they've been fighting with their content for some time, trying to organize it and get it down on paper. I encourage them to let go of this focus for a time, and instead center their efforts on defining the transformation their clients will get in words their clients can understand. Once the intended transformation is clear, they can ask people to register.

This is challenging because most people feel that they need to know *what they are going to do* on retreat before they can sell the experience. However, just like it's not necessary to know what a client's Sourced Experience be or how it will unfold, we don't need to know the "how" of our programming when offering a retreat. We only need to know that it will provide a Sourced Experience (meaning it is designed for clients to Release, Receive, and Rise), and what the Rise will look and feel like for our ideal clients and attendees.

When I can help retreat leaders see this and begin enrolling clients into their retreat, they suddenly find that content ideas start to bubble up out of nowhere! They are now present to the energies of the *actual* clients who will be coming (instead of the projected clients they were trying to attract through their "how.") Their magic begins to kick in to support their planning process, and everything gets easier.

Once their retreats are complete, many clients call or text me and say some version of the following: "Oh my goodness! That was *so* much easier than I thought it would be! I had my notes, but I only looked at them once! I knew exactly what to say, and even though I couldn't have planned for the things my clients were sharing, it was all perfect. I was *born* to do this!"

This kind of success happens over and over again. When leaders create the container for transformation according to the Anatomy, and invite the right clients in the right way, their magic simply appears.

Different aspects of my own magic have "come online" during retreats in unexpected ways. As an example, there was a time that I realized that the stomach pain I was feeling wasn't actually mine but belonged to someone else in the group. I had no idea why I was experiencing this sudden discomfort, but I got the nudge to ask, "Does anyone here have a stomachache right now?"

One attendee raised her hand. I asked a few questions about what was going on. Her sharing was unbelievable. This person had been sitting in the room grappling with her own truth, unable to see it clearly, but had not thought to raise her hand. We could trace the stomach pain to an early time in her life where she had "swallowed her words" and clenched her stomach, hoping that no one would notice what she was thinking. Through talking, coaching through the Two Truths, and validating the heck out of what was present, our shared stomach pain resolved rather quickly.

Then, there was the time I was hosting in Denver, Colorado. I went to my suite at the end of day two and sat down to make a list of each attendee and where they were in their transformation process by the end of that day. I had not yet developed The Anatomy of a Transformation at this point, so I would make notes about whether I felt that someone was in resistance (not yet committed), whether they were "ready to pop" or had "already popped," (meaning that they'd Received their Truth). I also made notes about what I felt they needed to see and do next to proceed with their transformation. (By the way, doing this for dozens of retreats is how I developed the Anatomy!)

On this particular evening, I reviewed the attendees and began to feel distressed. Most people were well behind where they would normally be at this point in the program. Many were still in resistance. Only a few had popped. Some would clearly refuse to pop in public, but the rest ... well, I just couldn't see how it was going to happen in time. I felt *so much responsibility* for their results. My energy field began to collapse with fear and despair. How could I possibly make up for all the transformational time I'd lost?

In that moment, something in me surrendered. I paused and asked myself, "What if, as you profess, anything was truly possible?"

I felt energy rise in my body. I said aloud, "If the Universe is truly abundant, then there is no lack of time here. I can trust that all of this will resolve exactly as it is meant to, in divine right timing." Then I reaffirmed my intention that most people in the room would "pop" by the end of the retreat, and I set my list aside.

My sleep was restless, which is unusual for me. I tossed and turned, waking up several times during the night. When I finally got out of bed the next morning, I felt that something important had happened.

When I walked into our retreat space an hour later, I swear to you that every single person *looked different*. It was as if

Source had woven magic with their energy overnight. When I did my morning check-in—which includes insights, a-ha's, and questions—I specifically asked, "Did something happen overnight? Who'd like to share?"

Most of the hands in the room went up.

All sorts of things had happened! Conversations with spouses. Spontaneous insights. New clients in their inboxes. It was miraculous!

I realized that I didn't need to worry or work so hard to hold space. There was so much going on beyond my personal "doing" that could source transformation. My energy and intention, in conjunction with the commitment of the participants, could work miracles.

In both of the above examples, I stopped, got present in my body, and listened to what was feeling True for me. I trusted my inner knowing—whether it showed up as a stomachache or an intuition to call in a miracle. My lovely strategic mind would *never* have been able to do that. And I certainly wouldn't have been able to let go and be so present were it not for my extreme clarity of focus at my retreats and my knowledge of the Anatomy (even if I wasn't yet calling it that).

ALLOW YOUR CLIENT TO RECEIVE YOUR MAGIC

When a client isn't making the progress you want, your audience isn't engaging, or one of your clients gets triggered in a way you don't know how to handle, you might start to spiral into thoughts like, "OMG, I'm failing. I'm not going to be able to deliver what I promised!" Then, when you reach for the magic, it feels even further away.

When you use The Anatomy of a Transformation as a foundational structure in your work, you never need to get caught up in your head, worry about what to do next, or feel like you're not enough. Instead, you can run through the Anatomy to pinpoint exactly where you are, where your client is, and what to do next to move the energy.

When used artfully, the Anatomy will *always* let you know the right time to bring out your best magic.

This is key, because using your magic at the wrong moment can strain relationships and utterly piss people off—or worse, drain and deplete you without you even noticing!

We've all had these moments where our magic just had bad timing. Like when you saw the exact reason why your BFF keeps dating the wrong people and shared it in the hopes of sparing her more heartbreak ... only to have her storm out of the bar fuming at *you*! If you had used your knowledge of The Anatomy of a Transformation, you would have recognized that, as much as you love your friend, she was not yet Committed to transformation. She never asked for your opinion, only your presence and compassion (and maybe your commiseration). Thus, your brilliant insight felt like an attack to her and caused her to push you away.

Or maybe you have a client who has not yet Released control and stepped into the "black box" of transformation. She comes to each call with a pre-conceived idea about what she "should" be getting. She wants to work on her social media strategy, but your Vibration Magic tells you that her current energy is attracting absolutely no one, and that no matter how much she "puts herself out there," nothing will happen until she transforms.

Week after week, you try to give her what she wants. She wants a strategy, but you see that it can be so much bigger and more aligned. And so, you tune in to your magic and "download" the best tagline ever for her aligned business. You excitedly share it—but it doesn't resonate for her, because she is not yet in the energy where she can Receive her soul-aligned copy. Now you're exhausted, and she's still feeling stuck.

This could also happen with a health coaching client who wants a "magic supplement" but isn't ready to look at her inner commitment to holding on to her weight. It may also occur with an executive coaching client who wants to transform her company culture but isn't committed to transforming her own toxic relationship to authority.

It's exhausting to try lead someone where they don't want to go. Unless they have Released their attachment to their old identity and become willing to Receive the Truth, they will not get the results they want. In such cases, you will need to go back to the Commitment step and work your way forward through the Anatomy again.

You will find that, if reviewed through the lens of the Anatomy, almost every instance of transformational frustration happens simply because you missed a step. You shared your magic *before* your client surrendered to the idea that your magic (and theirs) was more valuable than their control. If you backtrack to the beginning of the Anatomy, renew their Commitment, and hold them gently in their Release, your magic will be gracefully—and gratefully—Received.

MAGICAL TIMING

Your magic, whatever form it takes, is primarily used to reveal Truth. Therefore, the best place to apply it is when your client is ready to Receive.

You may also use your magic in earlier steps of the Anatomy. You may, for example, have a unique way of helping your clients get committed, or to feel safe to Release. But your magic really comes into full force when it's time to Receive.

As we learned in Chapter Four, the Commitment step does not need to be elaborate or unique, but rather a simple conversation to help your clients to see their desires and get present to their current discomforts. The Release step doesn't really require magic either, only that you have total certainty that it is safe for your clients to Release into the firm container you are holding for them, and that you communicate that certainty via the cues I'll share with you shortly in Chapter Ten.

Once your client is ready to Receive, now you want to work your magic!

Identifying the timing and context for your magic is an art as well as a science. You will need to become fully present *at will*, not by accident. You will need to test your magical process within the transformational framework of your offers. However, there is no doubt whatsoever that you will find your "groove," and start trusting yourself to Receive your own Sourced gifts in the most beautiful ways.

One of the easiest ways to support yourself as you perfect your transformational artistry is to create a business model and offers that lean into The Anatomy of a Transformation as a framework. This takes all the guesswork out of the various stages of the transformational process and allows you to step out of your analytical mind and into your flow no matter what is going on for your client.

Let me show you how.

CHAPTER TEN

DELIVER THE TRANSFORMATION YOUR CLIENTS CRAVE

*W*elcome to the strategy portion of your Sourced Experience! Here is where I'll show you exactly *how* to use your unique magic to create programs, retreats, and coaching pathways that consistently deliver the transformation your clients crave.

But before we get into that, I want you to notice something. The process I promised to share in this book—"How to Deliver the Transformation Your Clients Crave and Unlock the Magic You Were Born to Share"—was likely the reason you picked up this volume in the first place. But in order for you to use that process effectively, we needed to move through a Sourced Experience together! Now, from this higher energy and elevated understanding, we can implement the "promise" of this book faster and more gracefully.

You have Released your preconceptions about what transformation is and how it happens, and now you're ready to Receive new information about how to change your business to reflect your unique magic and the life-changing results you create for your clients.

Pretty awesome, right?

In the next two chapters, I'll share practical how-to insights in a few key areas:

- How to develop your business model and marketing to mirror The Anatomy of a Transformation.

- How to incorporate Sourced Experiences into your live and virtual work.

- How to feel confident in your skills and abilities to hold space for transformation.

- How to work with the various types of people who are drawn to transformational work.

While I will do my best to give you as much information as I can on these topics, my goal is to keep this book digestible. Plus, I know that once you start to Rise into this new energy of transformation, you will integrate these processes in a way that is totally unique to you—and not just a copy of my process.

(If you want to learn more details about these key elements, or integrate them into your cellular memory, please visit www. SourcedExperience.com/offerings to engage with our current offerings for Sourced Leaders!)

THE BUSINESS OF TRANSFORMATION

One of the core promises of our work with clients is to "Master the Business of Transformation."

Again, not all businesses *need* to be transformational. Sometimes people are simply seeking information. Sometimes they just want something handled for them. In fact, you may want to keep information and/or done-for-you products in your business even as you transition to a transformational model.

The Sourced approach is about the shared understanding that the "problem" your client wishes to solve is not simply an obstacle to their goal, but rather an *invitation to change.*

For example, a client's discomfort with their weight could be simply a "calories in/calories out" conversation based on information and discipline. It could also be an invitation to transform the root experience that caused the weight gain in the first place.

If a client has a desire to create a more profitable business model, there could be an information-based solution, with a course that explains the math behind increasing prices, client retention, and reducing expenses. This may be exactly what one business owner needs. However, the same profitability issue for another business owner could be an invitation to transform an internalized belief that has them continually making more money but failing to keep it, which is resulting in burnout. Transforming the belief first will help them to be ready to do the math later.

How many of your potential clients have been buying—or at least Googling—information-based solutions *for years*? And how many of them are still waiting for those promised results, even after implementing everything down to the letter?

When the person is ready for it, the right information will solve the problem.

But if their energetic state of being doesn't align with the results they want to create, no amount of information will help them.

I have a friend who's been struggling to get organized for … well, as long as I've known her. She's worked with professional organizers on several occasions to organize her space, but she's never able to maintain her clear, clutter-free space for long.

Like my friend, many people realize that information alone isn't working for them, and instead decide to outsource the solution. But even after investing even more money, they eventually go right back to where they started, because they haven't resolved the *energy* that created the problem in the first place.

Think of the business owner who takes course after course to learn to market herself but implements these strategies from her Default Energy (which includes a belief that these strategies won't work). When her efforts produce so-so results, she hires someone to market for her—but now, that marketing person has the impossible job of marketing on behalf of someone who doesn't believe that marketing can work for her. The business owner can't provide sound direction to her new team member because she's hoping the marketer will rescue her.

This business owner isn't doomed. She's not destined to go back to a regular job. She is most likely being invited to transform her deep-rooted beliefs around what it means to be visible as a business owner.

If you already work with clients to transform old, default energies—or if you are taking your work in that direction— this chapter is full of vital information for you. Even if you also teach brilliant information strategies, or provide done-for-you services, I invite you to create the sacred container for transformation *first*. Then, after the client has transitioned into their new Sourced Energy, you can teach the information and watch it "stick" in ways that were impossible before.

THE COMMITMENT STAGE: MARKETING & SALES

How many times have you been bombarded with messages like:

"Sales is the lifeblood of all business."

"Every day without sales is a day closer to going out of business."

"You're not actually a [insert business description here]. You're a *marketer*."

To me, information like this isn't helpful. It's designed to scare people.

The clients I work with aren't seeking more, faster. They're seeking lasting change. In fact, popular thinking about business and sales can make them feel anxious, instead of allowing them to trust the flow of clients and truly enjoy the abundant incomes they make.

That said, sales and marketing are *really* important. But because we don't need (or want) to buy in to popular thinking about hustle and metrics, we need to approach them differently.

Marketing and selling transformation is different than marketing and selling products, information, or other services. Your clients need (and deserve) a sacred container in which they feel safe to surrender. And so, you must hold your containers—your programs and offers—as sacred and offer them as gifts to the right people.

To create this kind of energy, your marketing and sales need to be about Commitment. Whether you're doing a Facebook Live to generate interest in your work, running a podcast, hosting a webinar, or creating your free opt-in gift, I invite you to begin asking the following question about your marketing: "Am I cultivating within my potential clients a commitment to their own transformation?"

In my first book, *Retreat and Grow Rich,* I shared a concept I call "Drawbridge Marketing," in which you invite clients into your "castle"—aka, your business—through strategic portals. The "rooms" in your castle are the parts of your work you wish to be known for, and the "drawbridge" is the marketing that invites your clients into those spaces.

My guess is that you already have some strategies in place around offering free content and list-building. This is great. However, your free offers need to invite potential clients to your email list (and your work) who *already have a burning desire for what you offer.* This is where Commitment comes into play.

I've run a highly-lucrative transformational business for over a decade now—but I don't have a huge list or a social media following in the millions. Instead, I have a list full of people who understand what I'm about and are highly committed to transformation as a pathway to their expansion.

This isn't by accident. While I am far from a perfect content creator (or business owner, for that matter), I know that my free content consistently cultivates the commitment to transformation. Therefore, people who don't believe in transformation and living Sourced don't make it past my initial lead magnet. However, those who *do* align with me sense that energetic match and want to know more.

DRAWBRIDGE MARKETING IN ACTION

My client, the ultra-talented Bonnie McVee, had been feeling pulled to base the core of her business around becoming fully yourself by transforming your relationship to God. "Once I am right in God's eyes," she told me, "I can give myself permission to be myself." This took some shifting, because her religious upbringing had instilled many ideas about a judgmental God who would smite her if she put a toe out of line. Transforming how she thought about God was life-changing for her, and as a result she wanted to help other businesswomen heal their own shame by transforming their relationship to God.

The issue was, she wasn't sure how to let others know what she was doing, or what she should teach in her free content. "How can I get the point across without overloading them with information?" she asked.

This is a common issue for transformational leaders. Their work is so nuanced and experiential that it is hard to "teach," or even describe.

Luckily, Drawbridge Marketing doesn't need to include a ton of teaching.

Bonnie and I developed a simple workshop structure. Her content consisted of sharing her own powerful story, and then guiding her clients to explore what they had learned about God through their religious upbringing. Specifically, they looked at the parts they agreed with, and the parts they didn't. Then, they built a list of beliefs about the "God of Their Own Understanding" from which to operate in their lives.

Next, she had them explore. "What has been the impact of holding on to the beliefs you were raised with but no longer feel are true? And what would be possible if you incorporated the new beliefs into how you run your business?"

And just like that, her workshop attendees were exploring their *commitment*. At this point, Bonnie could ask them point-blank how committed they were to transforming their view of God—and invite them into the container of support she had created for that transformation.

When you follow the Drawbridge Model, your offers are easeful invitations. You will never try to manufacture commitment by making someone feel bad about where they are, so it never feels pushy. The next step—the sale—is a natural outgrowth of your potential client's newly uncovered internal commitment to transformation.

Another example of Drawbridge Marketing is my Sourced Magic quiz. (If you haven't taken it yet, head over to www. ShiftTheField.com/resources!)

People love quizzes, right? But while quizzes give people information—in this case, what "type" they are—they don't always create Commitment.

My quiz provides people with a description of their Sourced Magic. It also invites them to an exercise to explore how much they are actually *using* said magic. Is it prominent or hidden? Are they charging appropriately for it?

The "answers" in my quiz help people explore what it would be like to transform their relationship to their magic—to help it become valid, valued, and visible. In other words, it gets them present to their discomfort about not owning (or even knowing) what makes them unique as a business owner, and their desire to manifest more of what they want in life.

I know that those who choose to move on to the next stage through my quiz are committed to transformation in the area of their magic. Nice, right?

I'll bet you can already see how and where you will want to tweak your marketing to inspire Commitment. Remember, it's not about proving how much you know, or sharing impressive information; it's about guiding your clients to explore their internal level of commitment. Once they're committed, you'll be able to blow their socks off with your magic!

Here are some tips for creating Commitment with your free content:

- **Share stories of transformation.** Share from the heart about your own journey. Your potential clients will begin to imagine what a similar level of transformation could look like in their life.

- **Speak to the discomfort and desire.** This helps people get present to their own commitment to resolving the discomfort and stepping into their desire.

- **Provide tools for them to evaluate their discomfort and desire.** Whether you are creating a quiz, an e-book, a webinar, or any combination of content, consider centering it around a tool for them to explore how content they are with their life today. Help them to get present to the desire that is really in their heart.

- **Bring presence.** As we discussed in Part II, presence is key when it comes to cultivating Commitment. You can do this whether you are in person or virtual. For example, on a webinar, pause with great intentionality as you ask them to reflect, ask powerful questions, and invite them to share their a-ha's.

- **Request Commitment.** Ask them to evaluate their own level of commitment. "If there were a solution that would bring you more of what you desire, and less of what you don't want, how committed would you be to that solution?"

- **Give them permission to *not* be committed.** Let them know it is okay if what you're offering is not for them! Doing this allows people who are not ready to transform to step away, and those who are to lean in. I often say something

like, "For some of you, this free training was all you needed. You got the nugget you were seeking today. Maybe this
helped you to realize that you *don't* want to host retreats or
live a Sourced life. If you take this self-knowledge with you,
I'd consider that a win."

- **Continue to create context.** As you teach, ask people to
  reflect on how what you are sharing relates to them directly.
  Provide prompts based on what you know would help them
  see how the "block" or Default Energy is present in their
  life. Ask, "How does what I'm sharing show up in your life?"
  "Do you relate to this?" or, "As I share this story, I want you
  think about a block that is present in your own life right
  now, a place where you've been frustrated."

- **Translate beyond the topic at hand.** If you teach about
  health, and they have found the gap between discomfort and
  desire around their health, have them translate that to other
  areas of their life. "How is this gap impacting you in your
  intimate relationships? In your work? In your parenting?"

- **Reiterate transformation first.** When I offer free content,
  I *always* speak to transformation first. If I am teaching a
  three-step process in a webinar, Step 1 will be about transformation. I let people know that, without doing the inner work of becoming Sourced, they will be implementing
  Steps 2 and 3 from the wrong energy. (You can also observe
  this in Part I of this book, where I remind you that, if you
  don't start from within, the information here won't be as
  helpful to you.)

- **Speak about investment as Commitment.** Let people
  know, up front, that their transformation is a committed
  process. Don't shy away from talking about money! Their financial investment represents their commitment, and their

transformation starts when they register. Even if someone already knows and believes this, having a verbal or written conversation about investment and commitment will solidify their commitment and begin the co-creation process of their sacred container with you.

WHAT ABOUT SALES?

People make sales seem really complicated, but in fact, it's simply a one-on-one conversation about the potential client's discomfort and desire. It's a discovery process designed to uncover the natural alignment that *already exists* between what your client wants and what you offer.

This is true for all sales and sales processes, but when your product is transformation, you need to find out not only what your client does want (aka, outcomes) but what they no longer want. You also need to confirm their understanding that, to achieve their desired result, they will need to shift how they show up and interact with the world.

Your clients are responsible for their own results—in life, and in the container you co-create with them. You are there as a guide to help them uncover how and why they've been creating the result they don't want, and to discover who they need to be to align with the result that they *do* want. As we discussed in Part I, you don't need to tell them how this will happen, or have the exact steps mapped out. You want them to Release their perceived control and trust your container and their own connection to Source—which cannot happen if your offer is too logical or analytical.

It's important that your client has an inner knowing that they want to go where you want to take them. It's also important that they generally align with your philosophies. If they've engaged with your Drawbridge Marketing, they will already know who you are and where your values lie, but with referrals this may need to be explained.

(Note: If you'd like to learn the exact steps I use to facilitate Sourced sales conversations, you can download my e-book, *"Sold Out Retreats and Transformational Programs"* at www. ShiftheField.com/resources.)

YOUR GATEWAY PROGRAM

There are many creative ways to design your business around transformation. The main thing to keep in mind is the Anatomy. This is exactly why I spoke to sales and marketing first: a committed client is the first step.

If your business model consists of one offering (i.e., private coaching) I recommend that you focus on marketing that helps people evaluate their commitment and leads them to a one-on-one sales conversation with you. For example, you could offer a free monthly workshop, where you share that you have a limited number of free discovery sessions available. In those conversations, you can discern whether their commitment is clear; if it is, offer them your transformational private coaching program. This is the simplest approach if you are just getting started.

However, many clients come to me when they are ready to expand beyond one-to-one work into group and retreat-based formats. In these cases, I encourage them to create a paid Gateway program to cultivate commitment among their ideal clients and weed out people who are not serious about their transformation. Even better, the Gateway Program takes the place of one-to-one sales conversations, saving you hours of time on the phone with those who just aren't "your people."

Your Gateway Program is an entry-level program, at an entry-level investment. It's often the first offer you will make after someone downloads your lead magnet or engages with your free content. In it, your clients will learn more about your approach, beliefs, and value system. They will also learn for themselves how interested (committed) they are to the approach and outcomes that you offer. The content can be super-valuable—for example, you could teach a condensed version of your full process for creating magical client results—but at its heart, this program is an exercise in examining their commitment, not the full transformational container you offer in other programs.

One of my gateway programs is my *Retreat and Grow Rich* coaching program. Most people who enroll in it have already read the book. In the program, I teach my entire system in as much depth as possible starting, of course, with transformation. I let people know that even though they will get a ton of information, they are likely to want additional support for their own transformation through my higher-level programs.

For some people, the course is exactly what they need. (For example, our client Candice took the information in the *Retreat and Grow Rich* Gateway program and turned it into a six-figure retreat business all on her own.) However, most people in the Gateway Program will feel pulled to take the next step with you. After engaging with your content, they will be present to the gap between their discomfort and desire and understand that there is something hidden from their view that you can help them to see. They sense that the Two Truths are ready to come to light.

While you might teach your entire system as your Gateway, I often recommend that your Gateway Program be a shorter experience which walks people through just the first step in your process—what I call "the first room in your castle."

After working with hundreds of coaches, consultants, creatives, and healers, I've discovered that the first room in their
castle almost always relates to cultivating Commitment! (No,
I didn't lead them there; it is simply what works!) They might
call this room *desire, vision,* or even *goal-setting*—but one way
or another, that Gateway is about Commitment.

Name and describe this Gateway Program in any way that
aligns with your brand and your ideal clients, but don't feel
the need to make this program super long or detailed. There is
great value in helping someone identify what they desire and
what they don't! There is even greater value in supporting them
to decide how committed they are to actually transforming
their life.

Your Gateway Program can be delivered live as a retreat,
workshop, webinar, or masterclass series, as a recorded lesson
or online course, or even as a one-on-one (this works well for
intuitive readings/assessments). Whatever you choose, be sure
that it gives people the space to explore what's happening in
their lives right now and get present to the gap. Whatever format you choose, be sure to include a module that helps them
get very clear that they are the ones in their own way (said with
no judgment and full compassion for our shared humanity).
Then, invite them to work with you further.

Sometimes a client will want to skip the Gateway step and
go right into working with you privately. Consider your stance
on this. You might require that they take the Gateway first, no
exceptions. Or, if someone truly wishes to skip it—if they hate
courses, for example—you might offer them an initial, paid,
session along with a detailed application. This is another way
to ensure Commitment.

There is nothing like the energy of a live, in-person group
and the ability to coach people in the moment. This is one reason to choose short retreats or interactive virtual programs as

Gateways. If your main goal is to create a consistent stream of pre-qualified clients who will be right for your high-level program or retreat, then be sure to include a live component in your Gateway. This can be as simple as including a free one-on-one implementation session with your course or creating a monthly group coaching call that is accessible to anyone who is actively enrolled in your program. I did this for several years with great success; the live Q&A calls were an opportunity for people to experience coaching with me in a group format, which helped them decide if it was right for them to come on retreat with me.

However, one of the main benefits of developing a Gateway Program is being able to "evergreen" it—meaning, people can buy the program at any time and the lessons will be automatically delivered. I have used several successful marketing funnels and evergreen program offers in my time as a business owner, but I'll offer this caveat: if your goal is to make a bunch of money on a course alone (without offering a higher-level program), hire someone who specializes in this. My approach is always about delivering maximum transformation with a secondary goal of automation.

My best advice for you when creating your Gateway Program? Keep it simple! Please don't go into over-delivery mode, and don't overthink it. Simply decide, "How will I let people see me in action with actual clients?"

THE SOURCED EXPERIENCE MODEL

The second step in your business model is The Sourced Experience! This is where the actual transformation happens—and, as

I shared in Chapter Four, it can be the most exciting, if not the most important, part of your work.

You can deliver your Sourced Experience offerings in a group setting or in a one-on-one. Some clients prefer one-on-one support because they are working with something deep and personal that feels too risky to share in a group. However, working with sensitive subjects doesn't rule out group work. In fact, part of your personal magic may be helping people feel comfortable sharing in a group! And, as we've learned in this book, group validation—especially during the Rise portion of The Sourced Experience—can be extremely powerful.

For many years, my business model relied on live retreats to curate Sourced Experiences. In 2020 (as I'm writing this book), the global pandemic gave me an opportunity to explore other forms of delivery more deeply, including virtual events and re-treats. These formats can work just as well—but I'll be honest, I've missed the energy of being together live!

You may also have recently been called to radically reinvent your business model. This is an exciting chance to get creative around the delivery of your Sourced Experience. However it looks, though, remember that this program level is centered around transformation or an energy shift. Your goal is to move your clients through the steps of The Sourced Experience. They Release their need to control, Receive their "Capital-T" Truth, gain insights around their "small-t" truth, and ultimately Rise into a new, Sourced Energy. At the end of this program, they will complete with the sacred container. They can then go out and integrate their new Sourced Energy into their life as they Rise or opt to continue with you through Integration.

The most important factor in designing your Sourced Experience is the power of intention behind the container. When you know that the goal of this program is for them to completely shift their energy, Source will conspire to provide the divine curriculum for this to happen in their life.

I repeat: Source will conspire to provide the divine curriculum!

This means you need to stop trying to control and overthink what happens in this program. You need to stop trying to get the perfect language or content. Yes, you may have a whole system, complete with beautiful workbooks and killer copy— but if you include too much training within The Sourced Experience, your content will get in the way of the transformation. Save the content for *after* their transformation when they are aligned and ready to absorb it.

It can be tempting to try to combine your Sourced Experience program with your Integration offering. This is certainly possible; a six-month private coaching program that starts with transformation and ends with Integration is a great example. However, in the long term, I recommend that you create a distinct offer focused around this massive transformation. On the other side of it, you offer your clients a next step to support the Integration of that transformation.

INTEGRATION: YOUR HIGH-LEVEL PROGRAM

After a retreat, I generally offer clients a next step in what I call my *High-Level Program* (HLP)—aka, my offer which supports clients in integrating their new energy or vibration. Generally, the HLP implies a high level of investment, both financially and timewise.

Because of this, you don't actually want all of the people who come into your Sourced Experience offerings to join your

HLP. You want to reserve this container for clients who have *already moved past their blocks* and entered a fabulous energy of flow and alignment. From this point, they are actually ready to implement what they have just Received through your Sourced Experience, and the rest of your wisdom.

So, what's involved in an HLP?

Your HLP is the most fun you can have with your clothes on! (No, really!) In an HLP, you will deliver your signature teaching and your highest brilliance. This doesn't mean you should hold back in earlier programs—but since you are focused on transformation first, you know that your clients will not be ready for the full scope of your information until they step into their new Sourced Energy. Once they step through that portal, you can dazzle them with your magic to your heart's content.

Once someone has been through The Sourced Experience with you, they "get it." They have the language to communicate what is really going on, rather than communicating with you from their wounded self. This doesn't mean they won't still go into low vibration; in fact, they are highly likely to do so as they integrate their transformation out in the world. But they are ready to be held accountable to the transformation they've chosen, and they trust you to help them navigate back to their Sourced Energy when they get derailed.

On the other hand, if you try to teach strategy and action steps to your clients before they are in their new energy, you will often find yourself backtracking and repeating yourself. Also, you will not have a common language with the client to be able to return them to a place of empowerment and possibility quickly.

Once again, in terms of program structure, I'm a big advocate for retreats (live or virtual). I often do two or three of them within a program and design each one with a different teaching that will help my clients integrate their transformation. My current HLP also includes virtual workdays where my clients come together and get a project done with the support of myself or a team member, plus their entire group who knows and sees them in their Sourced Energy. This is great because our Default Energy often creeps in around new or challenging actions; we've never taken actions like these before and we have a high desire to stay safe! When we work together as a group, there will always be someone to remind us of the transformation we are there to claim.

Of course, you don't need to design your HLP like mine. Your offering may be your one-on-one coaching, or even a personal VIP day or retreat. However, as mentioned above, there is true magic in doing this work in groups. If live retreats are not for you, please consider adding a group component to your HLP. This may simply be group Zoom calls twice a month, or high-level trainings that are delivered virtually only to clients at this level.

Most of all, your HLP should be *fun*. If the program isn't a joy for you to deliver, it won't resonate for clients, so spend some time getting creative about how you want to design your Integration offering.

SUMMARY: YOUR FULL TRANSFORMATIONAL BUSINESS MODEL

The full transformational business model looks like this:

1. **Drawbridge Marketing:** Free content that helps clients reflect on their discomfort and their desires and invites them to an initial Commitment.

2. **Gateway Program:** A paid program that continues to deepen the Commitment and helps clients decide if you are the person to guide them on their transformational journey.
3. **Sourced Experience:** An in-depth program (such as a retreat or an intensive coaching experience) designed to shift their energy from Default to Sourced.
4. **High-Level Program:** The program that supports your clients to integrate their new energy into their life.

Again, it's totally okay if you offer one comprehensive coaching program that delivers all the stages. Especially in the beginning, this is a great thing to do. However, after a decade of providing transformational support, I firmly believe that having separate programs at each stage allows clients to choose the support that is right for them, consciously opt in, and fully commit to what they personally need.

Many people will get what they need from your Sourced Experience program and move on. Some will only be Gateway clients. Others will do it all and perhaps even take your HLP more than once! (Note: when this happens, be sure that they commit to a new transformation in round two. You may even want them to take your Sourced Experience Program or even your Gateway Program again to help them decide what they are committed to for the upcoming year.)

I have been in all of the above situations as a client to other transformational leaders. I've worked with coaches in their Gateway Programs to gather information and decide on my level of commitment to the specific thing they teach. (In my case, specifically, I learned that I was not at all interested in creating a membership site. This was a very valuable use of $2,000, and I left the program both clear and grateful.)

At another time, I worked with a coach around a specific transformation I was seeking. I look back on the transformational work we did together with love and gratitude. The program I purchased helped me to get unstuck in a specific area, which made all the other work I was doing more effective. Yet, I wasn't sure this person would be able to help me integrate the new energy into my business.

And, in other situations, I've done transformational work with a coach and then gone on to hire them for Integration in their high-level one-on-one program or mastermind.

My goal is to demonstrate here that this is a beautiful, simple way to flow your business. It ensures that at each step of the process you are working with clients who are committed to what your program is intending to deliver. Most importantly, the design of your programs is set up to work with how transformation truly works in your client's life!

Remember that the main goal here is to teach your best stuff while at the same time providing a firm container of support for your client to navigate the particular stage of the Anatomy that is currently relevant to them.

So, what in this chapter is resonating for you? What are you now present to when it comes to designing your programs?

I hope it is something like, "This is *way* simpler than I thought."

In the next chapter, I'll distill my best practices for creating a curated Sourced Experience within your transformational business model. Whether offering a live retreat or a virtual experience, you can create maximum opportunity for them to Release, Receive, and Rise!

CHAPTER ELEVEN

THE ART OF TRANSFORMATIONAL EXPERIENCES

*T*hroughout this book, you've seen Sourced Experiences unfold through the stories I've shared about my personal experiences and those of our clients. In this chapter, I'm going to give you the framework for creating Sourced Experiences for your own clients.

As we learned in Chapter Ten, The Sourced Experience is something that you can deliver through an in-person or virtual retreat, or in a group or one-on-one coaching program—most likely in your mid-level program (between Gateway and HLP). It's the place where the Two Truths are revealed, and where your client will discover their new, Sourced Energy field and Rise into that energy.

There are five key elements to creating a Sourced Experience:

- A safe space to surrender
- The Truth-Revealing experience
- The Truth-Claiming experience
- Context
- The debrief

Each of these pieces is equally necessary to bring your clients through The Sourced Experience—from Release, to Receive, to Rise.

MAKE IT SAFE TO SURRENDER

Your clients will only become willing to Release control and open to their Truth if they feel they are in a safe space—meaning, a space where they will not be judged, shunned, or otherwise shamed for their "small-t" truth and the Lie they believed.

There are several ways to do this.

ESTABLISH YOUR AGREEMENTS

The first step to creating a safe space is to establish the *agreements of the container*, whether it is virtual or live.

Any time people gather, there are agreements in place about what is acceptable in that shared energy field. Most of the time these are unspoken, even subconscious—but they are always there. For example, when you walk into a beautiful, upscale spa, you know that you should be quiet to respect others' meditation and relaxation space. When you walk into a blues bar on a Saturday night, you know that the rules are completely different. You, and the people in both of those spaces, have agreed that the space should be held in a particular way. If you choose to behave otherwise, you may be asked to leave the space.

While many of your clients may understand what to expect from the safe space you're creating, many will not. Therefore, it's important to clearly communicate the boundaries of your space from the outset with clear agreements and guidelines.

One agreement that should be present in all Sourced Experience containers is confidentiality. Your clients should know that what they say in the container is held sacred and won't leave the space without their expressed permission (for example, a signed release form for their testimonial).

You may also add agreements such as:

- "I agree to participate fully."
- "I agree to be supportive of others."
- "I agree to ask questions and be open to feedback."
- "I agree to receive coaching and challenge myself to grow."
- "I agree not to coach others or give feedback without their consent."
- "I agree to hold a space of non-judgment."

There are many ways to phrase your agreements, and they should be consistent with your brand language. However, they should create a set of guidelines that all participants voluntarily agree to abide by. If an agreement is broken, as the leader you will hold them accountable and reinforce the container.

CHANGE THE TEMPO

In addition to your shared agreements, another beautiful way to get your clients to Release control is to hold an awareness of the pace and tempo of the container.

Allow this tempo to be a shift from their daily lives. This signals their nervous systems that this is an unusual situation, and that it's okay to try something different. Since our world is so busy and fast-paced, most often this means you'll want to slow things down in your container; however, for some groups, speeding things up will help them surrender. For example, if you have a group who loves to overthink, speeding up an activity may force them to release control and be more willing to receive support.

The slow-paced approach is something I did for a long time as "unconsciously competent"—meaning, I did it instinctively, without realizing how important pace actually was. Even if I know I have a lot to cover and my ego wants me to move quickly through the agenda, I understand that investing the time to allow clients to relax into the moment will help us move more quickly later.

SET THE TONE WITH YOUR MATERIAL

Opening a container with a vulnerable story from your own experience can be a beautiful way to set the tone for Release. You can even create layers of meaning by sharing about a time where you were called to surrender, and how that helped you transform an energy pattern that was keeping you stuck on your Old Tired Path.

Story is fantastic for two reasons. First, it gets people out of their own heads and creates a bond of compassion as they see your humanity and relate your story to their own. Second, it allows them to get to know and trust you more deeply as someone who understands at least some aspect of what they are going through.

Additionally, you can also simply *ask* people to surrender. You could create a teaching or exercise from your own unique magic that speaks directly to the importance of releasing control and trusting Source to guide their experience.

CREATE A TRUTH-REVEALING EXPERIENCE

After we've opened our container, established our agreements, adjusted the pace, and talked about the power of surrender, I like to offer an experience that helps my clients to Receive their Truth. On a live retreat, this may happen on the afternoon of Day 1. In a group program, this may happen in Session 2, or even Session 3.

The Truth-Revealing Experience will most likely involve something that feels out of control for your clients. This will allow them to have a different experience and open up to a new possibility. Most of the time, the client's ego/Default Energy will fight to stay alive, creating discomfort, resistance, and even anger.

For example, if a client's Default Energy makes it difficult to connect with others, they may struggle because a part of them wants to maintain a barrier to that connection. But if you have done the work to create a safe space in your container, and you have given the client space to surrender, they are highly likely to move through this discomfort instead of stepping away.

Remember Brittany from Chapter One? On her retreat, there was a team experience in which she played out the exact patterns she was experiencing at her job, and also in her family. She pretended to let another team member be the leader, then personally did all the work on behalf of her team! This was a Truth-Revealing Experience because it revealed a pattern that she had not previously been able to see. This pattern got in the way of her connection with others, and while it kept her busy, it didn't allow her to do the truly inspiring work she was born to do.

When you move into your Truth-Revealing Experience, be prepared for a multitude of different possible reactions. Some will have already started their transformation process, and so this experience will be taken in stride as they explore new ways of being right away. Others, like Brittany, will experience the contrast we've talked about. They'll get triggered by the experience, and their Default Energy will come out in a big way. Still others will get triggered but try to hide it, and then attempt to process in secret once the exercise is over. All of these responses are totally okay.

I like retreats because it's so easy to orchestrate an experience that's out of someone's comfort zone. When I do private retreats at my home or elsewhere, I create custom experiences that allow my clients to see how they are truly showing up and reveal that which has been hidden from their view.

You can facilitate these kinds of experiences in virtual spaces by including an element of surprise. The goal is to create a situation where their ego doesn't have time to plan out how they will respond.

We tend to prepare in advance for exactly how we will survive—and even win—at an experience. We love to do this before we even say yes to something, but even an hour's notice is long enough for the ego to do its work. Think about the last invitation you received, and the way you played out in your mind what would happen if you said yes, and what would happen if you said no. You probably wondered if you had the right outfit, if the setting would be comfortable, or if there would be people or situations present that you couldn't (or didn't want to) handle. By the time you made your decision, you knew whether you could survive the experience with your current sense of identity intact.

Transformation can't happen when we've already made a decision from our Default Energy about how to show up. In fact, transformation requires us to re-evaluate how we show up. This is why I love the element of surprise! Often, if people knew what they were actually saying yes to when they stepped into the container, they might have walked right back out again.

That said, there's no need for the experience to be extremely dramatic. Having people jump off a cliff, or get naked in a group setting, is definitely not necessary! However, the act of showing up to do anything they didn't anticipate in advance will bring the element of surprise. Don't underestimate the power of simple exercises—like eye contact, sharing vulnerably with the person next to you, or dancing in public—to really bring up that "out of control" feeling. These simple experiences can lead to deep awareness of "small-t" truths.

Here are some more examples of how to create Truth-Revealing Experiences in both live and virtual settings.

EYE GAZING

This exercise is best done in person.

Ask everyone to choose a partner (or if you're doing a private retreat, do this with your client). Then, have each pair stand arm's length apart, facing each other, and simply hold eye contact for one to three minutes or longer.

Sometimes, when I do this, I'll instruct people to look for the love in their partner's eyes, or the fear, or the joy. Sometimes they'll be searching for the part of their partner that reminds them of themselves, their parents, or another key figure in their life. This is often enough to help people hear the chatter in their head about themselves or the other person, and see the "small-t" truth that is happening there.

You can create a similar experience virtually by asking a client to gaze into their own eyes in a mirror.

IMPROV, DANCE, AND GAMES

I love inviting an improv instructor to guide a group through a series of exercises. Improvisation is a great truth-revealer! If someone isn't practiced with it, their Default Energy is sure to show up when they're asked to respond quickly in the moment.

Similarly, dance is a fabulous way to get people to notice their defaults. Do they trust themselves to move to the music, or do they hold back or even refuse to participate? Do they look around and copy others, or do they own the floor and do their own thing?

Games, too, require people to respond before they can think things through. I love creating games that don't make logical sense, or that are arbitrary with an unknown prize. We love to follow the rules, or break them, and our ego has created elaborate ways for us to keep our identities alive inside those rules. We might be the ultra-competitive one, the "enforcer," or the one who wants to sabotage everything to make sure we *don't* win. Creating a game that is essentially "unwinnable," or where the rules are constantly changing, will challenge every personality type and reveal the Default Energy underneath.

CONNECTION EXERCISES

Any experience that forces people to interact with others in new ways will reveal Default Energy.

For example, I've sent clients a Starbucks gift card with instructions to use it to buy a stranger's coffee. This is an experience that is far outside of most people's comfort zones. When I've done this, clients have found themselves analyzing who "deserved" the coffee, wanting to hide or buy anonymously, or even delegate the decision to the barista.

I've also created "people scavenger hunts" where clients go out into a public space and locate people who fit certain criteria— e.g., someone whose birthday is in the same month as their own, or someone who has a degree in finance. Especially if you instruct people not to disclose that they are playing this game, this exercise will challenge them around how they are showing up.

MEDITATION, BREATHWORK, AND GUIDED VISUALIZATION

Meditation, breathwork, and guided visualization exercises are great for revealing default energies and the parts of themselves clients don't want to see, especially for people who are normally super busy. There are literally hundreds of ways to facilitate these practices; use the ones that fit your own energy and modalities best.

I am guessing that, after reading the suggestions above, you are brainstorming ideas for experiences based on who your clients are and your area of expertise. Whatever you choose to work with, be sure to introduce it near the beginning of your program, any time after your safe space has been established.

THE TRUTH-CLAIMING EXPERIENCE

There's a second experience that I bake into my programs after the Truth-Revealing Experience. This second exercise is intended to move the client forward from the new, Sourced Energy which sprang from the recognition of their "small-t" truth.

Your clients have now Received their Truth and are ready to Rise into their new energy field. The Truth-Claiming Experience provides a loving pressure and opportunity for them to step into that new energy, fully claim it as their own, and be witnessed in their embodiment.

After your Truth-Revealing Experience, you will likely have various teachings, storytelling, exercises, and sharing moments with your client(s) to help them in their Receiving. The Truth-Claiming Exercise comes toward the end of your container, after they've had a chance to explore their new Sourced Energy field a bit. However, recognize that these two experiences—Truth-Revealing and Truth-Claiming—are keystones of the Source Experience.

You can make this second experience a repeat of the first one—only this time, your clients are approaching it from a new energy. Improv, dance, and eye contact are great for this; your clients can compare how they showed up from their Default versus their new Sourced Energy. Or, you can create an entirely new experience.

Here are some examples of experiences I've designed to help people claim their truth:

- The Declaration: Ask the person to come to the front of the room (or claim the virtual mic) and declare who they are in their new Sourced Energy. "I am Darla! I AM love, light, and freedom!" Support them to actually embody their declaration through the way they hold themselves, their tone of voice, etc. This may take a few tries, so be patient.

- The "Self-Expression Party": Encourage people to dress as an expression of themselves that they wouldn't normally show to the world.

- The New Business Story: Ask clients to give a short speech (three to five minutes) about their business story from their new energy.

- The Introduction: Ask people to walk around the room and introduce themselves to others from their new energy.

- The Vision Board: Creating a visual representation of how their new energy will show up in the world.

- The Deep Share: Ask participants to create and share a poem, song, or piece of art from their new energy.

Again, I trust that your creative juices are kicking in here, and that you are thinking of ways to create a Truth-Claiming Experience for your specific business or brand.

CREATING CONTEXT

Imagine that you've taken your group through the agreements, and then say, "Okay, now pick a partner and share with them something you've never told anyone. Ready, set, go!"

That request is going to elicit a base-level response. They may go through the motions of the exercise, but they have no idea what this exercise is intended to do, or why it matters to them.

Now imagine instead that you open with a heartfelt story about that time where you shared something you didn't even realize that you were keeping a secret. Sharing it helped you discover how that thing had been affecting you in many areas of your life, and how it had created a ripple effect that affected your work, your relationships, and even your body. Just letting the cat out of the bag made you feel so much bolder that you even asked outright for that promotion you'd been craving—and got it.

Then, you ask your clients to think about an area in their own life where they feel stuck. Ask them to write down the costs of staying stuck in that area, and the reason they'd like to break through that block.

Then, finally, ask them to do a partnered exercise called "Unburdening," where they share with their partner one thing that they have never told anyone. Let them know that sharing this thing is going to lead to their breakthrough in the area they wrote down earlier.

Can you see how this instruction will help them get more present, and take the exercise more seriously? This is also where Source comes in to play. When they have context for their thought process, they are highly likely to actually recall the story, thought, or event that will lead to their breakthrough!

When we did our photo shoot experience with Lori's group, which I shared about in Chapter Seven, I spent a fair amount of time creating the context the night before. I told them how to choose their clothing, how to show up, and how to hold the intention of revealing their true essence to the camera. Without context, that shoot would have been just another exercise.

Context creates the space for magic. You will want to create context before both your Truth-Revealing Exercise and your

Truth-Claiming Exercise, as well as for any other smaller exercises or activities you do in between. This will invite Sourced Energy into the space to allow everyone to get the most transformational "voltage" out of their experiences.

THE ART OF THE DEBRIEF

If context creates the space for magic, the debrief creates the space for Receiving.

The debrief is the most important part of any exercise, and happens after the exercise is completed. Having participants reflect on how they moved through an experience with an eye to discerning their Default Energy pattern will help them become aware of the "small-t" truth that has been hidden from their view.

I always ask clients to journal about what came up for them during an exercise before I ask them to share it aloud. This allows each person to share their Truth with themselves before they are influenced by the experience of others, or before they censor themselves to avoid judgments. I provide a series of journal prompts to help them through the writing process; they can use or skip them as they like.

Here are some of the journal prompts I've used in past debrief exercises:

- When I first described the exercise, what was your initial response? How did you feel, and what were your thoughts about the exercise?

- What were your thoughts about ME when I first gave you the exercise?

- How did you approach the experience initially?

- Did your strategy for making it through the experience change over time?

- What did you notice about how you showed up?

- Would you say that you showed up the way you normally do, or did you show up differently? If so, how? Why?

- As you did the exercise, did any person or specific experience trigger you? (In other words, did something make you angry, annoyed, resistant, shut down, etc.?) If so why? Who/what did that person or situation remind you of?

- What was the area of life you wanted to transform when you joined this program? How might the way you showed up to this experience be impacting your results in that area of life? Other areas of life?

- What do you want to celebrate about how you participated in the experience?

- What would you want to change about how you participated in the experience?

- What belief are you noticing guided how you showed up in the experience? As you reflect, is that belief actually true, or is it simply something you were taught? What could you believe instead?

- What is your main insight from this experience?

If the exercise involved working with a group or team, you can also use prompts like these:

- What was your initial reaction when you got into teams?

- What did you like about your team? What did you not like?

- What role did you play in the team? How is this similar to the role you play in other areas of your life? In what ways were your teammates similar to other people in your life?

- Did the team dynamic change over time? Why or why not?

- In which ways was this the perfect team for you?

After the client finishes journaling, you can ask them to share their insights with you and/or the group.

If you are in a group, you may wish to use one of more of the following approaches:

- "Popcorn sharing." Ask people to raise their hands (or even shout out their responses). This is a great time-friendly option.

- Paired sharing. Ask them to pair with someone in the room (you can do this virtually by using the "breakout" function in your meeting software) and share according to specific prompts. (Note: I usually have a few people share by "popcorn sharing" after a pair exercise, so I can get looped in on where they are. Paired sharing is a nice option when you sense that everyone in the room really needs to be heard by someone.)

- Around the room sharing. If the group is small enough (6-7), I may have each person share.

Sharing is where the "gold" is for your clients. It's also where the art—aka, your magic—comes in to the debrief.

In *any* transformational program, even if it involves large groups, individual sharing and coaching will be responsible for the most significant "a-ha's" and breakthroughs across the group. When one person moves through a transformation, it opens up Sourced Energy in the space. Several other people will shift at the same time—either because they have the same patterns in their own lives, or because the energetic opening allows them to hear their own version of their Truth.

Truth has a frequency. When it's present, there's no mistaking it.

In the optimal flow, you'll have them capture their insight in their notebook, then have them share with a partner, and then have a few people share with the room.

In this last portion, you'll need to decide what to do with their sharing. This is where your presence and deep listening come in, along with your unique Sourced Magic.

As each person shares, you can decide to do one or more of the following:

USE A WHITEBOARD/FLIP CHART

I often end up with an unwieldy number of flip chart papers at the end of a retreat, but it is worth it. It is super powerful to see words written on a flip chart. Sometimes, the exact words that someone shares are the *exact same words* that will lead to their breakthrough. Seeing them in writing is so helpful!

VALIDATE AND MOVE ON

Always use one or more forms of validation when someone shares. (I talked about how to do this in Chapter Seven.) They got the insight, they shared it. You witnessed their sharing, let them know they were heard, and affirmed that the insight they expressed was valid. In some cases, that might be all that some-one needs to move through the Rise and into Integration.

QUESTION THE SHARE

Sometimes, clients will try to stay in their Default Energy throughout the reflection process. Their mind will convince them that they are seeing it clearly, so as to protect them from seeing the "small-t" truth. This happens frequently—and it's ex-actly why they need to show up and ask for support. For some reason, they are unable or unwilling to see it on their own (like when I talked myself out of exploring my sexuality).

When someone shares an insight, and your "Spidey-sense" (aka your magic) kicks in to tell you there's more to the story, you may choose to question the sharing. There are many skills to employ around this, but a good example would be asking, "Does that feel true to you?" "My intuition tells me that there might be something deeper here to think about. Do you agree?" or even, "I noticed during the exercise that you were the last one to leave the room, but that seems different than what you are telling me now. What do you make of this?"

Never make someone wrong or challenge their sharing in a way that feels shameful. However, don't be afraid to give them something to think about, or remind them of something they said earlier that will help them go a layer deeper.

USE LASER COACHING

Some of the sharing in your container may lead to what I call "laser coaching." This is when you coach someone individually to have a breakthrough in a group setting.

In this scenario, you will apply your magic to help the individual discern their Two Truths, distinguish the new, Sourced Energy that they want to own from now on, and create an assignment for them to experience that.

In most instances, you won't have time to laser coach everybody in the group, so trust your intuition around who to work with in this way.

Some indicators that it's time for laser coaching:

- They've shared a profound insight and you know it will be simple (and incredibly helpful) to take them to the new Sourced Energy because they are so ready.

- Their sharing indicates that they are missing the mark on their insight and they need some help to see their Two Truths clearly.

- They are not yet through the Release stage, and your coaching will help them to surrender control.

- They ask a question that shows you they are grappling with seeing their Truth clearly, and you know you can support that clarity.

The goal of the laser coaching is to distinguish the "small-t" truth, the "Capital-T" Truth, and the new Sourced Energy. Mastering this takes time, so be patient with yourself. Remember, everything is Sourced!

GIVE OUT ASSIGNMENTS

If someone's sharing is telling me that they haven't quite gone deep enough yet, it's possible that they're not yet Committed (or that they need to recommit). In these cases, I'll give the person an assignment to explore their commitment. (My favorite is the Cost-Benefit T-chart I shared in Part II.)

If the person simply needs to spend more time with their insight to truly anchor it, or if the schedule simply doesn't allow me the time to coach them, I will give them a simple assignment to explore further.

Some examples of assignments are:

- "Journal about the impact of this."

- "Look over your calendar for the last two weeks and explore how many times you did [insert behavior]."

- "Ask three people in your life whether they see you as [insert descriptive word]."

As you can see, these exercises will be personal to the individual and require you to engage your unique magic to move them forward. (Remember, you've already done the Truth-Revealing Experience or Truth-Claiming Experience; this is a way to take an individual deeper.)

(Note: Want more support in looking to your clients with an eye toward Truth? Download my short paper, "The Cast of Characters in Your Retreat Room" at www.ShiftTheField.com/resources. It's super helpful even if retreats aren't in your toolbox right now!)

GO FORTH AND TRANSFORM!

It's time to celebrate!

You have all the tools to design your business in a way that will consistently create transformation for your clients! You've unlocked your unique magic and learned how to move your clients through The Anatomy of a Transformation with intention and grace.

So ... now what?

As you know by now, I believe that the way we create alignment within ourselves is to step into a powerful container of support. I create these containers for my clients, and I receive them for myself.

I often joke that my goal is to work myself out of a job. In a Sourced world, there is no need for coaching containers, because we all speak a common language of love. However, in today's world, we need firm support for our Truth-based magic to emerge, because it just isn't the "norm" yet.

If you are supporting others' transformation, you need support for your own. Not at every minute, of course; I know that I've found great value in grounding my integration for a time after completing a program or container. But in general, I find it invaluable to my work to be in a continual, supported process of uncovering my "small-t" truths and integrating my Sourced Energy.

The programs that my company offers are designed with the application of practical magic in mind. We will support you to further develop your magic, while applying it to your unique model of business and transformational leadership. After all, transformation doesn't happen in a bubble, but on the court of life!

I'm thrilled that our transformational experiences offer the best of both worlds—spiritual and practical—so that our clients can allow their expanding Sourced Energy to touch everything they do and create. I hope to see you in one of them soon!

AFTERWORD
A WORLD, SOURCED

I was leading a retreat in New Orleans when I discovered
something about my willingness to be "publicly Sourced."

The group had just come back from our Truth-Revealing Experience. We'd moved through our debrief process, and I
could feel the room processing. I had a few ideas for next steps;
I'd written my intended next exercise on my agenda (personal
reflection and partner sharing), but I also had a thought in my
head that it might be good to move some energy through dancing or some other physical movement.

As I rolled these options around in my head, the fifteen people in the room were watching me with anticipation, wondering what unexpected thing I was going to ask them to do next.

"One moment," I said. "Just take some deep breaths with me."

I put one hand on my belly, and the other hand on my heart.
Breathing with the group, I asked Source which direction was
right in that moment. Within another few breaths, I knew exactly what to do. Surprisingly, it was none of the options I'd been
evaluating in my head. Instead, I got the hit that I needed to take
a few more insights, a-ha's, and questions from the group.

Several people shared additional insights from their experience. Then, one woman asked, "Just now, I saw you stop to check in with yourself about what to do next. What would you do if you needed to check in, but you were *in public*?"

I laughed. I wasn't sure how much more "public" I could be than standing in front of a room full of people who were all staring at me! But I loved how her question clearly reflected the intimacy I'd created among our group.

However, as I considered her question, I realized something: I had become the kind of person who would have no problem stopping to "tune in" publicly! It was something I had hoped to embody—to live so attuned to my gut knowing that my life always worked out beautifully. Certainly, each time my life appeared to *not* be working out, I could trace it back to a decision which had not been run past my inner knowing.

"I'm thrilled to say that I would behave exactly the same way 'out there' as I do here," I finally replied. "Imagine how fabulous the world would be if all of us did this!"

Think about a world in which each human being was one hundred percent responsible for accessing their own inner knowing about what was right and aligned for them—without getting blocked by the confusing messages of past experiences, without old inherited energies or traumas from their family of origin, without society's list of acceptable behavior patterns in the way. How fabulous would it be if each human being was energetically clear and aligned, fully present and embodied, and speaking their Truth from the heart?

In such a world, no one would withhold their Truth to stay safe. No one would fall back on "small-t" truths to manipulate a situation. No one would go along to get along because it was easier than speaking up. No one would carry baggage around how they expected others to respond to them. Instead, we would all be fully ourselves and able to come together to create something fun, expansive, and impactful simply because we could!

In this world, we would give ourselves the experience we actually came to this earth to have! We wouldn't waste time trying to control where our life was going. We wouldn't live in the past wishing that we had done things differently, nor would we live in the how-to's of the future. Instead, we would create from within the present moment—expressing, connecting, and loving in exactly the right ways for our personal Sourced journey.

Dear reader, this world *already exists.*

The population of this world is small, but rapidly growing. Its doors are open to you. The invitation has been extended.

But to live in that world—a world where you can be "publicly Sourced"—you need to choose a Sourced way of life.

You need to become willing to surrender into the Sourced Energy that you already are. More, you need to know with complete certainty that Source has your back, and that when you follow your inner guidance, all will be taken care of.

BELIEVE YOURSELF, RECEIVE FROM SOURCE

When my best friend told me that I should refrain from telling people I was gay, just in case I was wrong, I can still remember the whole host of physical sensations that fired off in my body. I felt tingly and tight, a bit nauseous, and utterly terrified as I read her email from my seat inside a retreat I was attending, designed to help me find my marketing message.

For a fleeting moment I let her feedback sink in and I thought, "What if I change my whole life for this … and I'm wrong?" I immediately wanted to crawl in a hole.

Then, I paused, and began to reflect—as I do as a perpetual Truth-seeker.

I remembered that I was in charge of my Truth. *I* got to decide what fit for me. I revisited my unmistakable physical response to kissing a girl for the first time.

The resonance of Truth was unmistakable.

That led me to reflect, "If my dear friend thinks she's entitled to an opinion about something as personal and intimate as my sexuality, where else are people sharing opinions that are inaccurate, and even harmful?"

As is everything we experience, her question was part of my divine curriculum. During a break, I scribbled down my thoughts in my journal. On one line, I wrote the words, *Believe Yourself.*

I was clear that this was not the same as "Believe *in* Yourself." That overused phrase feels to me like one of those bad affirmations that keep you stuck on your Old Tired Path and remind you of all the things you think you're bad at.

But *Believe Yourself* rang true for me. Believe your inner knowing. Believe in the world and the life you want to create. Believe that your ideas are valid. And most importantly, believe that the messages you received from your inner knowing are as "real" as the thoughts in your head or the words on this page.

We don't get confused because we don't know the answers. We get confused because *we don't believe ourselves.* We listen to the "good advice" of our family members, the "experts" in our business fields … even the friends who tell us we aren't gay.

Within ten minutes, I committed in my notebook to birthing a new message. And so, the "Believe Yourself Challenge" was born. I ran this challenge live a few times in the following year, and I also turned it into an evergreen program that my clients could access. I brought forward tools for hearing your own inner knowing and highlighted the ways that doubts are sown that keep us from owning our magic.

That challenge was my Drawbridge Marketing at the time. Hundreds of people signed up to participate, and many went on to purchase my other programs.

Today, as I operate under the Sourced™ brand and distinguish what it means to be Sourced, the words "Believe Yourself" are as true as ever.

To believe yourself is a prerequisite to receiving from Source.

Each of the Sourced Magics we explored in Chapter Nine come with a prerequisite: You must *believe that what you are perceiving is real*. For example, if the Universe gives you signals—you see 5:55 on the clock every day, or a hummingbird shows up in front of your window three days in a row even though you've never seen one there before—listen. You are noticing these things for a reason. It's Source tapping you on the shoulder. If you don't believe your inner knowing that these signs are meaningful for you, you will miss the message.

The more we believe what we see, feel, and know, the more we will Receive.

Source isn't something that is "out there" doing things "to" you. Source *is* you, and you are Source. We are all part of the same collective consciousness expressing in different ways as distinct souls. Therefore, we can't look outside of ourselves for answers because others' answers are for them, and their distinct soul paths.

You may find pathways within others' containers, offerings, and counsel—but your answers will always come from within.

WHEN WE RECEIVE, THE WORLD WORKS

I never expect anyone to believe me or just blindly take my word on something. In fact, that would be counter to what I just wrote—and what I teach all my clients!

I have a belief about how the world works; I'm sharing it with you here. However, don't take my word for it! Run this past your own inner knowing to see how it resonates. Tune in and ask, "Does this feel true for me at this time?"

When we open our connection to Source, believe our inner knowing, and act on it, we will receive the exact guidance we need to make the world "work" for us. Meaning, we will receive all the abundance, experiences, resources, connection, ease, and joy we need to walk the path we've been given. There will be no lack. Even in the most difficult of circumstances, a path will appear for us. If we can hold ourselves in love and light and not take the process too seriously, we can find our way to the alignment that is available.

This is the way out of disharmony. Individuals will no longer feel the need to accumulate resources as protection against a harsh world. Balance and equality are restored. There's no need to justify or save face for past actions; instead, we can own our past fear-driven actions and transmute them to a higher form without judgment. Violence is no longer a symptom of the "small-t" truths we have believed. All of life can be held with loving presence.

In her work, my friend Lisa talks about how we can co-create with Source to bring about "Heaven on Earth." I agree. All that is occurring is Sourced and is available to guide us back to

Source and the place where alignment happens and everything just ... works.

TINY PILLARS OF LIGHT

When my soul connects with the highest vision of my work, I see tiny pillars of light all around the world. They represent all the humans like you and me who are waking up to this new way of living and leading.

As each light grows brighter, it reaches out to connect and intimately link with the lights of others on similar journeys. This collective "net" of light strengthens and grows more complex over time, until it looks like a mirror of the Milky Way.

Many Sourced leaders have come before me, and my vision for humanity is nothing new. However, I am holding space today for this future in which light leaders around the globe become connected in ways that empower their work and embolden this public, visible display of Truth.

Imagine if there were politicians in this "light leader" network. Media personalities. Fortune 500 CEOs. It's happening! Soon, a whole new language will be introduced to this collective vernacular. The old energies that have been leading nations will wake up and realize that the "underground" network of light leaders are no longer underground, and that they actually have the energetic and economic power to transform the globe! This network does not rule with fear, power-over dynamics, or a drive toward accumulation at any cost. This network is powered by Source. It honors Mother Earth and all Her creatures. It honors Spirit, and all the ways we intersect for a collective vibe of light, love, and freedom.

Thank you for engaging in this work and giving me the opportunity to share this vision with you. If I can shine a light on *your* light during this journey here together, I would be honored. And most importantly, thank you for who you are in the world … already, as is.

I love you for walking this walk. The world needs your magic!

RESOURCES

To support you in the process of delivering the transformation your clients crave while unlocking the magic you were born to share, I've developed some specific resources I think you'll love.

Go to www.ShiftTheField.com/resources to access ...

- **The Anatomy of a Transformation Cheat Sheet**
- **Our Sourced Magic Quiz**, the perfect way to discover how your unique spiritual gifts can serve your clients
- *Sold-Out Transformational Programs*, an information-rich, experiential e-book
- **The Retreat and Grow Rich Experience Library**, a master list of ideas for creating Sourced Experiences
- **Links to our YouTube channel** where you'll find ongoing educational content

... and more to be added as this work grows and evolves!

ADDITIONAL SUPPORT

- Work with us in our magically Sourced business coaching programs or become a Certified Sourced Leader. Explore current openings at SourcedExperience.com/offerings
- Hire one of our certified coaches or retreat leaders at www. SourcedExperience.com/sourced-leaders

ACKNOWLEDGMENTS

I'd like to acknowledge the special people who supported me in writing this book, starting with my wife, the beautiful Kimmi Ward. Thank you for the mornings and evenings in which you didn't have my full attention because this book came first—and for your transformational magic that is both a container of support for my best self and a challenging provider of contrast, all at once!

Thank you to my team at Sourced, especially Janet Kodish and Julie Flippin who held down the fort for me as I attempted my first draft. To Shennel Shakes, Mimi Tran, and Manda Stack, who kept my schedule light during my editing process. To the seventy-some-odd humans who joined our "book study" and read along with me as I wrote this. And to Veronica Wirth, whose Vibration Magic and design skills held the space for this book cover to emerge (and so much more!).

Thank you to the magical healers, bodyworkers, and coaches who helped keep my physical and emotional bodies aligned as I let these words come through. I've never felt so supported!

Thank you to Pat Verducci, my writing coach: you always asked that perfect question that made me go, "Hmm ..." and made my writing soar. And to Bryna Haynes, editor and publisher extraordinaire: thank you for your immediate belief in this book, and all the ways you made it better.

Thank you to my clients, especially those whose stories lie in these pages. You chose me as your transformational guide and teacher. You are my why, and I know I'm *so* on purpose when I witness who you are in the world. Our collective impact matters. Stay magical as we raise the vibration of this planet together.

And finally, thank you to my animal friends, real and imagined. To my dog Monty, who left the planet during the writing of this book after sixteen years by my side; and to Sir Oswald Cobblepot, the newest member of the family, who stepped in and held it down just after Monty's departure. Thank you for licks and butt wiggles, which are sometimes just what the writing doctor ordered! And to that mythical creature, Pegasus, whose feather appears on the front of this book. Thank you for guiding the unfolding of the Sourced brand, within which people learn to live the life they were born to live without restraints or fear of judgment. Where they step into their highest vibration, aligned with the essence of who they truly are, doors of possibility open wide!

ABOUT THE AUTHOR

Darla LeDoux is a transformational business coach, "recovering engineer," the best-selling author of *Retreat and Grow Rich*, and the founder of Sourced™. Since 2009, she has guided thousands of clients to confidently market, sell, and deliver deep transformation, unlock their own magical Sourced Expressions, and build lucrative businesses based on deep energetic alignment.

Darla is committed to doing business in alignment with what feels right to her soul, because she's learned that, "What our soul wants is always the most practical thing we can do." She envisions a world in which all people access and live by their inner knowing, making it valid, valued, and visible in their most magical work.

After years of following others' formulas for success, Darla reclaimed her Sourced connection—critical for leading in the way that works for her. With a unique blend of business expertise and intuitive healing magic, she supports her clients to not only understand nuanced business strategy, but to more importantly hear their own soul's guidance.

As the creator of the Sourced Leader certification program, Darla equips her clients with the structures and tools to lead their own clients through the process of transformation with the deepest integrity. Graduates demonstrate mastery at shifting the field in their own and clients' lives, creating a whole new playing field for how we "do" life as a collective.

Darla's companies have generated millions in revenue, selling transformation first, strategy second. She's been featured on stages of many coaching industry leaders, as well as a plethora of podcasts and online events. She hosts Sourced with Darla LeDoux on YouTube, and The Retreat and Grow Rich Podcast on iTunes.

Prior to starting her business, Darla graduated with a BS in chemical engineering from the University of Minnesota and held senior roles in marketing and product development with Procter & Gamble. She resisted the call to the world of coaching and transformation for ten years until a death and divorce helped her find the courage to follow her soul's desire. Her third of three coaching certifications was obtained through iPEC coaching, whose mission she still aligns with today—raising the consciousness of the planet one human at a time.

Darla lives with her wife, Kimmi, and fur baby, Oswald, in Austin, Texas. You can learn more about her work at www. SourcedExperience.com.

ABOUT THE PUBLISHER

Founded in 2021 by Bryna Haynes, WorldChangers Media is a boutique publisher of transformational nonfiction.

Our focus is "Ideas for Impact." We know that great books can change lives, topple outdated paradigms, and build movements. Our commitment is to deliver superior-quality transformational nonfiction by, and to, the next generation of conscious entrepreneurs, changemakers, creatives, and industry disruptors.

Ready to write and publish your thought leadership book with us? Learn more at www.WorldChangers.media.

Made in the USA
Coppell, TX
12 April 2021